E=M

Soldier of peace
DAG HAMMARSKJOLD

Britannica Bookshelf — Great Lives for Young Americans

Soldier of peace

DAG HAMMARSKJOLD

by Burnet Hershey

Photographs courtesy of The United Nations

Published by
ENCYCLOPAEDIA BRITANNICA PRESS, *Chicago*

TABLE OF CONTENTS

Secretary-General Hammarskjold in front of the UN buildings

Chapter 1

The Shy One Holds the Stage

There was nothing theatrical about the career man, Dag Hjalmar Agne Carl Hammarskjold, except in his private life. Close friends tell about the time he sat atop the Swedish mountain Suliteima declaiming poetry for hours on end.

In his professional life the second Secretary-General of the United Nations was almost fanatically dedicated to being inconspicuous. He chose to practice a conscious split of himself. Dag, the Secretary-General, was not the personal charmer who could twinkle with a boyish unpredictability. Dag, the Secretary-General, was Sphinxlike, formal, impersonal, brilliantly intellectual, with scarcely a trace of levity.

But on the historic day of October 3rd, 1960, the fair, tall, slender Swede cast a magnetic spell over his audi-

At his desk in his 38th-floor office

ence. In his quiet way, he upstaged one of the biggest scene stealers of all times, Nikita S. Khrushchev, Chairman of the Union of Soviet Socialist Republic.

The scene took place at that modern palace of glass in the heart of New York City, the United Nations building. Television viewers all over the world were able to witness a piece of unrehearsed, uncensored history in the making.

The immediate live audience was composed of almost one thousand delegates to the United Nations,

[8]

representing ninety-nine nations. They were assembled in the International Theatre of the General Assembly for the UN's fifteenth yearly meeting. The delegates had traveled from far-flung points of West and East. Their political and social beliefs were those of the democratic and communist worlds, the neutral nations, and the recently born African states. Never before in history had the heads of so many different nations gathered in one place.

Dag was seated behind a high marble desk on the platform. Surrounding him were men and women of ebony, brown, coffee complexions, and white-skinned representatives from Britain, Western Europe and other northern climates. Men and women from Senegal, Somali, the Chad, Vietnam, Thailand, Mali, Yemen, from the infant African nations with strange-sounding names, were displayed in a blaze of their native garbs. They wore turbans, skull-caps, sugar loaf hats, Homburgs, and snap-brim felt hats. They wore snow-white burnooses, flowing mantles and robes, vari-colored saris, and heavily bejeweled earpieces.

From high in the dome of the General Assembly's massive hall, camera lights targeted on this representative body of world citizens. Dag Hammarskjold's fine-stranded hair was sand-colored under the electric lighting. The faint suntan on his fair complexion was washed out by the lights. He wore a conservative, well-cut business suit. Only the softly blended tones of his bowtie and the clear blue of his eyes displayed any color.

[9]

This Fifteenth Session had opened according to a prescribed agenda. The first order of business was to elect a president for the General Assembly. One by one the delegates were delivering an overwhelming majority to Ireland's Frederick H. Boland. As Khrushchev cast his vote, he displayed a flamboyant "thumbs-down" gesture over the ballot box – a gesture intently viewed by the well-mannered Dag.

The votes were counted, and the dry-witted Boland was inaugurated as President of the General Assembly. His first task was to make official Declaration of Admission to the United Nations of no fewer than fourteen nations. The entire balance in the UN was changing, since at this Fifteenth Assembly, the number of African nations had reached twenty-three. Their presence in the world organization might serve to alter the overpowering weight of the Soviet Union delegates and their Red orbit satellites. Communist leaders might no longer find it possible to upset easily the global boat with the bloc of their votes.

The number of countries now a part of the UN was almost double the number of member nations in 1945. With the addition of delegates, the UN had the increasingly awesome responsibility of trying to maintain world peace and justice for some two billion people.

The first speech on the agenda was given by the President of the United States, Dwight D. Eisenhower. He committed the U.S. firmly to active support of the UN's purpose . . . peace throughout the world, preservation of

[10]

freedom and justice, humanitarian and educational aid for underprivileged peoples everywhere.

President Eisenhower recommended, that the United Nations be given the power to carry out its plans in Africa; that, when necessary, forces of member nations be placed under United Nations command; that there be inspection of atomic weapon production; that the United Nations supervise the peaceful control of outer space. . . He offered from the United States not "pounds" but "tons" of fissionable material to be used for the peaceful production of atomic power in underdeveloped lands.

Such projects, supervised by the United Nations, would make the UN the most powerful body on earth. Dag Hammarskjold, its Secretary-General, would thus become a kind of International Chief Executive.

President Eisenhower left the General Assembly Hall, to tremendous applause, for a hasty plane trip back to Washington.

The President's departure was Khrushchev's cue. The next day he stormed up to the rostrum and delivered one of the most bombastic speeches in his tempestuous career.

Khrushchev spoke in Russian, and his words were simultaneously translated into English, French, Spanish, and Chinese. During his two hour and twenty minute monolog, he disdained subtlety and concentrated on shock value.

"Dag Hammarskjold, the Secretary-General, is a

fool!" "The United Nations is just a part of the United States State Department . . . and President Eisenhower is a liar . . ."

"I demand," Khrushchev thundered, "that we appoint a three-man Secretariat to replace Dag Hammarskjold!" Sensing that his audience was neither convinced nor captivated, Khrushchev rambled on in wilder, freer style.

"The Secretary-General has tried to justify bloody crimes against the Congolese people," the Kremlin boss charged with furious indignation. "It is improper that such a man should hold such an important post . . . I demand that the Secretary-General should muster up enough courage to resign . . ."

Khrushchev cocked a trained ear and stood at the rostrum waiting for applause before returning to his seat. There was only a tortured silence from the stunned multitude, until member delegates from the Soviet Union's captive nations came to Khrushchev's rescue with vigorous hand-clapping. There was Janos Kadar of Hungary, nicknamed by Hungarian freedom fighters as "the butcher of Hungary," because his armed tanks had exploded lead into thousands of Magyar rebels. Rumania's Gheorghe-Gheorghiu-Dej chimed in to strengthen Kadar's applause, as did Bulgaria's Todor Zhivkov, Albania's Mehmet Shehu, and Czechoslovakia's Antonin Movotny. Poland's Wladyslaw Gomulka applauded the loudest and the longest. There was applause from these and a few other men, but the rest of the assembly sat silent.

What had gone wrong with Khrushchev's spectacular show?

"The script was just too unbelievable," one television reporter recalled. "You could sense that Khrushchev had offended too many intellects. He had dampened spirits, he had smothered hopes for settling the cold war. Mainly, he had ludicrously attacked the integrity of perhaps the most tireless, capable officer of the United Nations, Dag Hammarskjold."

Even the heads of delegations friendly to Russia looked blank, disappointed, and bewildered throughout the Khrushchev address. They had expected him to act in a reasonable manner. Instead he had called for the removal of Secretary-General Dag Hammarskjold, and had hurled vulgar name-calling not only upon Hammarskjold but also upon United States policy and its Chief Executive.

Among the world leaders who were hoping for good things from Khrushchev was Prime Minister Jawaharlal Nehru of India. Though a world traveler in his youth, he had lately become reluctant to leave his native land in these troubled days. At first he had declined to attend this Fifteenth Assembly. He decided to be present only when Khrushchev told him that he was coming. Nehru sat motionless, his face wearing a look of calm detachment as he gazed upon Secretary-General Dag Hammarskjold during Khrushchev's address.

Whatever might be said of Nehru's political philosophy and his patience with transgressors in the arena of world freedom, he passionately stood for peace. Nehru knew that the selfless, gentle-spoken Swede, Dag Hammarskjold, was unswerving in his life purpose to keep the world from war. One of the things Nehru must have remembered, as he studied the lonely figure of Dag Hammarskjold, was that the Secretary-General had well earned his unofficial title of The Peacemaker. Hammarskjold was forever globe-trotting to sore spots around the world; he was always on call to try to settle disputes in his objective, logical, but humane and understanding way. Four years earlier he had admonished France, Britain, and Israel for their warlike Suez expedition of 1956. In that year of 1956, Hammarskjold had threatened to resign if these countries used force to attain their ends. And now, with a record of distinguished dedication to peace behind him, he had been *asked* to leave his post.

Throughout Chairman Khrushchev's onslaught against him, Dag Hammarskjold had listened, his face an impassive mask. From time to time he jotted notes.

It was more than risky that Khrushchev had laid bare a vehement antagonism toward Dag Hammarskjold without attacking the United Nations Charter itself. He had upheld the Charter against the Western powers who had put forward his name for the job, and against the Communist powers who had seconded his nomination in 1953 and again in 1957.

The men and women in the Assembly auditorium stirred with embarrassment for Hammarskjold's humiliation as he rose to reply to Khrushchev's demand for his dismissal.

[14]

Dag Hammarskjold folded his hands tranquilly before him. He spoke thoughtfully, in a softly disturbed tone.

"It is very easy to resign. It is not so easy to stay on. It is very easy to bow to the wish of a big power. It is another matter to resist . . ."

Mr. Hammarskjold's statement was interrupted by a spontaneous roll of applause from his fellow statesmen. He looked surprised for a moment, then encouraged.

"By resigning, I would . . . at the present difficult and dangerous juncture of affairs, throw the organization of the United Nations to the winds," Dag explained, making it clear that it was not so much he, as the world peace body which Khrushchev wanted to destroy. . . . "I have no right to do so," he said in the simplest terms, "because I have responsibility to all those member states for which the organization is of decisive importance — a responsibility that overrides all other considerations."

Again, a resounding burst of applause spilled over the Assembly. Members from the newly born African states arose and clapped loudly to show their faith in the Secretary-General. Khrushchev became so angry that he pounded his fists against his desk in protest.

Dag Hammarskjold, the self-effacing, quiet one, had captured the spotlight. He continued speaking in even, unemotional tones, but with steadier assurance.

"It is not the Soviet Union," he said pointedly, directing his remark to the new nations, "nor indeed any other big power which needs the United Nations for its protection; it is all the others. . . .

"I shall remain in my post during the term of my office [until 1963]," he concluded firmly, "as a servant of the organization, in the interests of all those other nations, as long as they wish me to do so."

His brief retort to Khrushchev was stated in unadorned, plain language, so that no one could miss its import: Dag Hammarskjold was not bowing to the bluster of one man's whim—not when it meant the possible disintegration of the United Nations.

The assembled world leaders showed their hope and confidence in the Secretary-General by giving him a standing ovation.

This dramatic spectacle in the UN seemed even to affect people outside the building. Police on duty along the United Nations grounds reported they had never had such a troublesome day. Escapees from Iron Curtain countries demonstrated in disorderly fashion, trying to break through the barricades to demand freedom for their countries. They protested against dictatorship and the wholesale slaughter of their countrymen. They wanted to speak to Khrushchev, to boo him, they said; they wanted to talk to the puppet leaders of other Red orbit nation. Emotions were at fever pitch.

Later that evening, at a social event in the Soviet Union's Park Avenue embassy, Khrushchev greeted Hammarskjold with a broad grin and a warm handshake, much to the discomfort of Dag who had accepted the invitation as a matter of diplomatic politeness.

Hungary's Janos Kadar was overheard asking Khrushchev, "Why the bear hug for Hammarskjold?"

Khrushchev's answer came in the form of one of his innumerable store of aphorisms—an old Caucasian Mountain saying: "A man is your friend while under your roof sharing your bread and salt." "However," Khrushchev emphasized, "this does not preclude your slitting his throat once he leaves your house."

Chapter 2

Yesteryears that Made Today

Ⅰt was the evening of July 29, 1905. Inside the Villa Liljelholmen, in the lake-side town of Jonkoping, in the province of Smaaland, south central Sweden, there was more excitement than usual about an oncoming addition to the Hammarskjold family. There hadn't been a new birth in more than five years.

"I *do* hope you will grant us our *fervent* wish, Dear Lord...."

Agnes Almquist Hammarskjold gasped for breath in the midst of her prayer. She knew the baby, her fourth child, would be born within a few hours, maybe less. Devoutly, she prayed to God to give her and her husband, Hjalmar, their first daughter.

"I want a little girl who looks just like you, with your merry eyes," Hjalmar had told her, in one of his rare expressions of tenderness and praise for her beauty. Agnes had melted with pride, recognizing that this is what most husbands say when they love their wives. It was good to know Hjalmar still loved her, after fifteen years of marriage.

Throughout the Hammarskjold residence, the household help, generally calm and orderly, were dropping things and speaking in loud, unrestrained voices. Miss Erna, the family nurse, was seated downstairs in the main room, flushed in anticipation of the helpless life to be entrusted to her care. The senior Hammarskjold, whose brain was usually so filled with worry about the fate of his country in war or peace, allowed himself to think about the coming arrival. He sat stiffly and impatiently in his study, waiting to be summoned at the end of Agnes' labor to welcome the new offspring.

The youngest son, Sten, an exuberant, lovable child, somehow sensed that a great deal of attention would hereafter be given to the baby, and the thought made him fidgety and uneasy. Would he see even less now of the mother he adored, who had not enough time to play with him and listen to his thoughts? She seemed far away from him these days, daydreaming and talking about the wonderful sister he might have. What would a sister be like? Who cared about a sister when he got on so well with his brothers, Aake and Bo?

Bo, the eldest, had experienced the eventfulness of two previous births. He tried to explain how simple it was to his youngest brother. "Sten, mother will be in pain and

[19]

then the baby will wish to relieve her of her suffering, so it will come into the world, and then you'll see it's nothing at all," he said smartly. Aake, who had been around for Sten's birth, echoed: "Sure, Sten, you came here the same way, and *I* looked at you and you were red in the face and crying."

The three boys had a laugh over this, which was all but drowned out by loud thunder that suddenly rattled the windows. The children ran to the terrace windows and gazed down upon Vatter Lake. The faint light of the misty-ringed moon gave them a hazy view of battering waves and a storm-tossed sky.

"It's good luck when a baby is born in a summer storm," Bo said.

"Why?" Sten asked.

"That's what they say," Bo replied authoritatively.

Good luck or not, twenty minutes later the baby made its entrance. The mother, overanxious about the sex of the infant, stubbornly held on to consciousness until the doctor told her whether she had her girl.

"It's a beautiful, perfect boy," the doctor said, smiling.

"Oh," she whispered in disbelief, and fell into a deep, exhausted sleep.

In the summer of that year, 1905, when Dag Hjalmar Agne Carl Hammarskjold was born, no amount of sunshine could thaw the cold war that froze out harmonious relations between the rulers of Sweden and Norway. An artificial union which existed between these two nations threatened to erupt into war. The crisis had been slowly growing since the end of the Napoleonic wars, in 1814, when Sweden emerged with the possession of Norway as a prize. It seemed long overdue that, in order to preserve peace, the incompatible union be dissolved and Norway granted her independence.

Hjalmar Hammarskjold, distinguished public servant and expert in international law, was chosen by his country to be Chief Arbitrator in the dissolution negotiations. As President of the Gota Court Advisors — the Jonkoping Court of Appeal — and Minister of Religion in Prime Minister Christian Lundeberg's cabinet, he was believed the man best able to succeed in the quest for peace.

Hjalmar Hammarskjold, in fact, was so immersed in mapping a strategy for preventing war that he was rarely at home and had little opportunity to play with his new son.

"Hjalmar, don't you love our new boy? Did you really want a girl so badly?" Agnes blurted the words out one night when her husband came home late and didn't even peek into the dimly lit nursery.

"Foolish woman," he chided her gently, "he's a fine little man. I'll get to know him very well, soon, when all this is over," he said with a preoccupied sigh.

"Our Dag really is very precious," Agnes beamed. She had become less disappointed about not having a girl in the family when she saw how creamy-complexioned, deep-blue eyed, and adorable this infant was.

The baby Dag, who slept so soundly and uncomplainingly in his cradle, was innocent of the man-made turmoils and triumphs of the world into which his parents had introduced him.

What does a baby dream about, except images of fear and comfort, hunger and pain, of which he cannot yet speak? While little Dag had his tiny head propped on a delicately embroidered white and blue pillow, important things were happening in the world around him.

In Russia, the Grand Duke Sergius was assassinated, signaling the first rumblings of the Russian Peoples' Revolution. The Japanese fleet under Admiral Togo had destroyed the Russian Navy, and shortly afterward a peace treaty between Japan and Imperialist Russia was signed in an American Navy yard at Portsmouth, New Hampshire. In America, the colorful Teddy Roosevelt was exercising a strong presidency, and Wilbur Wright had just made another successful airplane flight, a full 38 minutes aloft. An earthquake all but destroyed San Francisco.

New industries were springing up as a result of new inventions. Great new fortunes were being accumulated by resourceful individualists, such as America's Carnegie, Ford, Rockefeller and Scandinavia's Alfred Nobel. Color photography, moving pictures, scientific and medical discoveries, machine technology, an emerging Germany, the Socialist Revolution, and dictatorships, were creating newspaper headlines.

The Victorian period, which was more "Victorian" in Sweden than in the Queen's own land, was drawing to a close, and the "Gay Nineties" of European high-life, which started in Paris, was just reaching the capital of Sweden. Ibsen, Strindberg, Anatole France, Flaubert, and Zola were the literary and theatrical rage, and Kaiser Wilhelm of Germany was the royal glamour boy getting ready to play his sinister role.

Three months after Dag had taken his place in the Hammarskjold household, Aake asked his brothers, Sten and Bo, "For heaven's sake, when are we going to christen Dag?"

"Let's ask Mama, " Bo suggested bravely.

Agnes Hammarskjold was resting in her bedroom dressing room when she heard the timid knock on the door.

She was nervous and impatient lately. She told herself she had no right to feel unhappy about the fact her husband scarcely saw her except to say, "Good morning, Agnes," "Good night, sweet one." After all, he had lived all his adult life by the ideal of duty to his country first, and personal duties and pleasures second. She understood this loyalty and devotion, yet sometimes it was impossible to be content about it. She was not a demanding woman, but she craved the presence and attention of her husband.

"Oh well," she thought to herself wistfully, "I suppose one day all my sons, too, will leave me to love their

[23]

country *first* . . . I had better be happy with my little ones while I have them around me . . ." She thought about the healthy, pink-faced baby, Dag, and felt a glow of motherly delight at the remembrance of how chubby and cuddly he felt when she held him to her bosom.

"What is it ?" Mrs. Hammarskjold said with a start, hearing the unexpected knock at the door. She hoped it might be Hjalmar.

"It's us," she heard Bo's voice say. "We wish to speak with you, please, Mother." In a formal request, Bo said "Mother," but, under ordinary circumstances, he and the other boys called her "Mama."

"All right, if it is important," Mrs. Hammarskjold said. "Wait five minutes and then you may come in." Though she was not a pretentious woman, Agnes' Hammarskjold was most meticulous about being properly attired and well-groomed at all times, even in the presence of her children. It would take her five minutes to get off the chaise lounge, straighten her gown, and run a comb through her wavy hair piled neatly in a high bun at the back.

Precisely 300 seconds later, by Bo's small gold vest pocket watch, the children entered their mother's quarters.

Mrs. Hammarskjold sat on the bed and her sons seated themselves in chairs facing her.

"Now, what is so important, dears?" she asked.

"We want to know please, Mother," Bo said, the blood rushing to his cheeks and ears, "why our baby brother

[24]

does not yet have a name. That is, why we haven't had a real christening for him, like with Sten and Aake and me."

Mrs. Hammarskjold had trained her sons to abide by the laws of the church and the dictates of society. She was glad to see how well-ingrained this teaching was.

"I am pleased you ask about this," Mrs. Hammarskjold said. "I can assure you that neither your father nor I have forgotten about your baby brother Dag, and that he shall be christened very soon. It is just that your father cannot spare the time just yet to be here for such a sacred event—but we *shall* have it, you will see!"

Was it prophetic that Dag Hammarskjold's christening rested upon the interests of peace from which his father could not be distracted? "Peace." More and more, it became a household word in the Hammarskjold circle.

The christening was possible, at last, in late fall, after the September Karlstad peace delegation had met with the Norwegians. Hjalmar Hammarskjold had presided, as major mediator, together with a committee of his peers: Prime Minister Christian Lundeberg; Minister of Foreign Affairs Fredrik Wachtmeister; Consultant to the Swedish Government Karl Staaff. They had confronted the Norwegians at the conference table with goodwill and in a spirit of negotiation. The mediators agreed to grant Norway her rightful sovereignty. The bitter disagreements faded. Hjalmar Hammarskjold felt free to go home for a "reunion" with his wife and children.

The tension of delicate diplomacy had been lifted

from the senior Hammarskjold's mind and heart. For as long as it might last, he threw himself into the totally different and pleasurable position of being husband and father. To the great joy of Agnes Hammarskjold, he planned the belated christening party of their youngest with zeal and good humor.

"We'll invite all our dear friends," Hjalmar promised her, and they did, some 35 of the country's leading statesmen, scholars, lawyers, clergymen, including of course the Lutheran minister who performed the rites.

"See, I told you your brother would have his proper blessing," Mrs. Hammarskjold said privately to her sons, as they gathered around for the ceremonial.

Bo, Sten, and Aake were not terribly interested now that the affair was actually taking place, but they did look forward to extra cakes and the wee measure of wine they were allowed to have afterwards.

For the gurgling, wide-eyed, four-month-old Dag Hammarskjold, there was a deluge of gifts: bejeweled knee-length spats for when he grew older, plush angora sweaters, exquisite lace nightwear, and many other articles of apparel which elegantly dressed children then wore.

A messenger had arrived toward the end of the celebration, bearing a joint gift from the Prime Minister and from two other noted members of the Karlstad peace delegation. The Hammarskjolds, slightly overcome, eagerly unveiled the gift. It was a gorgeous cup of gleaming silver imprinted with the name: Dag Hjalmar Agne Carl

Hammarskjold, and below it was the sentiment:

FOR THE TOO LONG NAMELESS

Christian Lundeberg   *Fredrik Wachtmeister*   *Karl Staaff*

Everyone laughed at the dedication: "For the too long nameless," and little Dag, the center of attraction, was squeezed and kissed by his elated mother and father.

In Agnes' and Hjalmar Hammarskjold's eyes there were tears of faith in the difficult life they had chosen to lead. At this moment, especially, they believed in its sweet compensations. "A *peace* cup," Hjalmar Hammarskjold kept repeating. "My son is surely a born peacemaker, as God willed it."

Nearly two months rolled by with a steady level of happiness. Even the minor accidents which sometimes develop into tragedies did not touch the Hammarskjolds.

For example, when Nurse Erna put Dag in the carriage for a stroll in the park, young Sten, who had become very fond of the baby, asked to go along. "He's so cute," Sten told the nurse. "I want to help you watch him." Erna agreed, and with Sten along, parked the carriage and slipped away for a brief walk in the rose garden. When she returned, she clutched her throat in anxiety. Sten had climbed up on the carriage to look at his brother, but he bent over so far that his weight tipped it, overturned it, and both he and the baby lay sprawled on the ground, much to the horror of the conscientious Erna.

Fortunately, there were only a few cuts and bruises

to show for the spill. Much later, when Erna had courage enough to confess what had happened, her understanding mistress said with equanimity, "My Dag is proving already that he will be able to withstand hard knocks and survive very well, which is very important in this trying life."

Just as it seemed to Agnes Hammarskjold that family life was settling down into a comparatively stable routine, Hjalmar Hammarskjold abruptly announced he had been appointed Ambassador to Copenhagen.

"I must leave immediately for this post," he told his wife, "and after I get settled there, you and the children and Nurse Erna will be able to follow me. I'm so thankful for this new opportunity," he added with a far-away look.

Mrs. Hammarskjold knew what that look meant. Her husband was detached from all family ties as of this moment, and *she* didn't matter much, nor their four youngsters, compared to the "duty above all" which he forever preached.

"Hjalmar," Agnes Hammarskjold said, trying to hide her fears of new loneliness, "it's so wonderful. I'm enormously proud of you, dear . . ."

The next morning Ambassador Hammarskjold was in Copenhagen. It wasn't until several months later that his family were able to join him.

The ambassador's career and stature soared so rapidly that in 1907, scarcely a year later, he was designated governor of Uppland province. The family moved again, this time for a long, long stay, into the red brick Vasa Castle in the town of Uppsala. There Dag Hammarskjold's first remembrances began.

Uppsala . . . The senior Hammarskjold's early memories went back to Uppsala, too. As a ten-year-old farm boy from Vaderum, he had gone to this university town determined to shed his impoverished background and to make something of himself. In 1878, he had been the number one boy scholar among the pupils graduating from Cathedral School. That had been the beginning. He had earned a professorship in law. To return to Uppsala, after almost thirty years, as governor, flooded his mind with nostalgic thoughts, and filled him with zeal for new, higher attainments in the service of his country.

Governor Hammarskjold was fiercely proud of his heritage, poor as his people had been. Hammarskjold (meaning "hammer and shield") was a name which had for centuries meant that the Hammarskjolds were serving king and country. The first Hammarskjold to serve, Peder Mikaelsson Hammarskjold, was knighted in 1610 by King Charles IX for "valor in battle." The governor reflected on these fragments of the past and he thought: "For me, I hope it shall always be 'valor in avoiding war,' unlike Charles who was rather an opportunistic politician . . . . ."

It isn't every child learning to toddle around who grows up in a governor's castle and has magnificent historical walls on which to scrawl chalk marks and

[29]

crayon doodles – when his mother and father are not looking. But this is what Dag did during those explorative pre-school years. His doting, good-natured mother never spanked him for it. Instead, she would do something would teach him a lesson. Agnes Hammarskjold would brush Dag's hair until it would crackle with electricity.

Mrs. Hammarskjold had let Dag's golden, wavy hair grow to shoulder-length curls, an optional custom in that time for both boys and girls. His hair was so richly silky and shiny he had been nicknamed "Goldilocks" by Mrs. Hammarskjold's lady friends, who loved to stroke it, much to the child's wild dislike.

"No, no, Mama!" Dag would shriek when his mother brushed his hair, or when strangers touched it. Ordinarily, he was a model of obedience, but this he could not bear.

It was no use. He had to wait until he was of school age, when Papa insisted his hair be cut, and that the frequent hair brushings be ended. No longer would Agnes Hammarskjold be able to adorn her youngest son in frilly bonnets that matched his gorgeous hair, nor would she be able to caress his springy long curls.

"Auntie Hildur" was the name of the grade school where children started their education. Here Dag was initiated to reading, writing and arithmetic; every subject, in fact, except German, which he was taught by private tutor at the castle.

The baby Dag, who had been so cheery and smiling,

had a reserved personality now. He did not smile much, out of shyness, for a smile is an outward invitation to friendliness. Perhaps it was because he had not yet made friends with other boys. His brothers? They considered him a baby still, and had nothing much to say to him that made sense. Papa? Papa liked to talk to Mama and to their grownup friends but not much to him. Mama? She was wonderful, everything in the world, and she read beautiful-sounding words to him from poetry books, but Mama was not a boy to make friends with.

Instinctively, the reticent young Dag realized that it was up to him to solve the problem of finding someone. This aggressive attitude, which was contrary to his nature, gained for him a boy friend his own age, Jon Olof Soderblom, son of Sweden's newly appointed Archbishop.

"We are going home by the same way, you and I," Dag forced himself to say to Jon Olof one day after class had been dismissed. This was not so, actually, because the Archbishop Nathan Soderblom and his family had not yet moved into the official residence below the road from the Hammarskjold castle. Repairs were still under way and had delayed the family's getting settled.

Dag had made the first move, however, to welcome Jon Olof's companionship. He was trembling that he might be refused, but the other youngster very happily joined him in a stroll home.

"We'll be close neighbors, soon, and we'll be friends, won't we?" Jon Olof asked openly. He was a warm, pleasant child, full of enthusiasms.

[31]

Dag blushed and they shook hands on their pact of friendship. It was a marvelous day.

Dag and Jon got along well together. Dag was mentally precocious, but did not have an outgoing personality. Jon had a quick intelligence, too, though he had to study harder to master his lessons. Dag, it seemed, could daydream half the classes away and then know what Miss Akselson, their teacher, had told them. He seemed to do his homework without effort. Jon loved to talk and make broad gestures, and Dag depended a great deal on this companion to counterbalance his own shyness.

The two boys shared a kindness in their natures. Miss Akselson taught classes from a wheelchair, and Dag and Jon decided to be extra nice to her because she could not walk or run. They often stayed after school in order to wheel Miss Akselson out of the class room to where she waited for her transportation. The disabled woman, a very independent, happy person, was extremely gratified to have these softhearted youngsters, who were her best students, paying special attention to her.

"And what are you going to be, young men, when you grow up?" she asked Dag and Jon one afternoon.

Jon answered, "Like my father, the Archbishop."

After only a second's pause, Dag answered, "Why, a school teacher, of course, Miss Akselson, like you."

Seeing how happy this made her, Dag would tell her over and over again that he would be a teacher, until he finally believed himself that he would, and he would talk out loud to his imaginary pupils.

[32]

Then next year, and for years after that, Dag's passionate interest was collecting butterflies, beetles, bugs of all sorts, and stuffed birds. In his huge playroom on top of Vasa Castle, there were rows and rows of specimens, some in jars, or under glass, looking as vital as living creatures, unlike the army of stiff toy soldiers strewn about the room.

"Soldiers fight and kill people, and they're not so smart because they get killed, too," Dag told his chum Jon, as he shoved his foot over his prone toy soldier, General Ingmar. "Look how dead he is," Dag said, making believe the soldier had been slain in battle.

"If you don't want your army any more, I'll take the soldiers," Jon said brightly.

"No," Dag retorted after thinking it over. "I might need them. But they're really not much fun."

Agnes Hammarskjold, now addressed as Madame Hammarskjold, predicted proudly to her guests on an afternoon as they sat having tea, "My Dag will be a great biologist one day." Present were the wives of well-known statesmen and educators who had gathered to discuss some civic activity. Now, however, their conversation had lapsed into womanly talk about their families.

"Oh, do bring the boy up and let us hear some of his bright chatter," one of the ladies suggested.

Dag was summoned to bow to the ladies and to kiss their hands, as his mother had taught him to do.

As the women gushed their approval of young Dag's courtly manners, Mrs. Hammerskjold said, not realizing

[33]

how ludicrous it sounded or how it would offend her boy, "You know, the Governor and I have always been sorry we never had a daughter — but Dag has been just like a daughter to us. . . ."

Dag controlled his tongue, though he felt like yelling, "Mama, how *could* you?"

"Were you studying some flower or insect life just now?" one of the ladies asked Dag.

"Yes, M'am," Dag said, and instantly withdrew from his pocket a live, big beetle which he impulsively deposited in the terrified lady's lap.

His chagrined mother, amid apologies, swiftly escorted him from the room. Before she could scold him, Dag, who already knew how to use words to his advantage, turned his agonized little face up at her and said, "If you had a *daughter,* she'd play with *dolls.*" Then he dashed upstairs to be alone.

"He's gentle, but he can't be stepped on, thank God," Agnes Hammarskjold thought to herself when she realized she had been at fault.

When Dag reached the age of nine, he was transferred to the same school as his brother Sten, which brought the two boys closer in thought and spirit than the older boys, Aake and Bo, who were attending schools of advanced learning. Sten, though more than five years older than Dag, had tremendous admiration for him because of his brilliance in school. As an adult, Sten recalled in his autobiography how easy it was for his brother, even

[34]

as a very young student, to embarrass the teachers by asking them logical questions which they could not answer.

"I can see Dag wearing his dark blue sailor's dress, shaking his solemn blond head while hearing a discussion on the chameleon. Miss Ragnhild Berglund, our teacher, told us how the chameleon changed its color, from brown to green on a green base, to hide its presence from an enemy. Dag suddenly put up his hand and asked, 'Miss Berglund, do you know what will happen if you put the chameleon on a spotted surface?' No, Miss Berglund didn't know the answer to that, but Dag volunteered an answer. 'It will break apart,' he said matter-of-factly and with a touch of merriment."

At home Sten and Dag relied a good deal on each other to escape loneliness, until Sten would weary of a nine-year-old's talk, clever as it was, and each would go alone to his room. It was only with the advent of a royal visit, or a holiday, that the entire family would be together in an atmosphere of informality, fun, and spiritual unity.

Dag never forgot his part in hosting King Gustaf and Queen Victoria. It was Dag who was asked to put away his nature collection and toys to make his room fit for Queen Victoria to sleep in.

A royal visit always meant some members of the family had to share rooms. The twenty-five rooms in Vasa Castle were hardly enough to accommodate the Hammar-skjolds and their household staff, let alone royal visitors and their numerous court. To complicate matters, on this particular visit, Queen Victoria did not feel strong enough to join in the gala banquets, but preferred to eat alone in her room — Dag's room.

The candid governess had told Her Majesty that her youngest charge had been pleased to give his room to her. Queen Victoria thereupon took a great liking to Dag and allowed him to enter her room and be with her while she dined. Dag looked on with big eyes as this finest of ladies sat in his room. Behind her special chair was a lackey dressed in green velvet. A footman, his wig flying, ran back and forth from the downstairs kitchen to the room, carrying dish after dish of piping hot food. Queen Victoria did not seem at all sick to Dag as she ate this seemingly endless procession of meats, fish, vegetables, and fruit.

Usually, during a royal visit, Dag and Sten watched the splendid parties through moth holes in the plush, but old, draperies. (Aake and Bo were considered old enough to join in the festivities until a certain hour.) This time Dag was the most privileged of all, and he reported to Sten what the Queen looked like, and what she did and said.

The morning after the Queen's departure, to Dag's extreme delight, he was handed a thank-you note by the Queen's messenger, signed personally, "Victoria."

It always seemed to Dag, who craved his mother's presence so much that he would follow her around silently, that his mother was forever doing things which had nothing to do with him, Bo, Sten, or Aake. Dag was right about this. Mrs. Hammarskjold was so anxious to help others that sometimes she neglected her own sons.

Agnes Hammarskjold never heard anyone was ill without sending a get-well greeting. If she heard of a person needing food or shelter, she would immediately dispatch money and other help. She was constantly active in political, religious, and educational circles. And she was always overworked by personally handling a voluminous correspondence.

In one of her letters, written in 1914, to Mayor Johan von Bahr, one gets an idea of her involvement in the world around her, her warmth, and her devotion to her husband:

"I feel ashamed that I did not write right away to thank you for your help and kindness, but Austria's declaration of War toward Serbia occurred on July 24, and President Poincarè's visit on the 25th, after which the whole tragedy that the world is now witnessing [World War I] took place piece by piece, and day by day, and Germany's declaration of war came on August 1st, and the first general mobilization of Sweden on August 2nd . . . Hjalmar, and the Minister of Defense had immeasurable work and responsibility, worries and anxieties — anxieties which I shared with him, as everything . . . all the telegrams and everything that had to be done was concentrated around our telephone night and day, and all other thoughts were swallowed by this alone . . ."

Before he was thirteen, Dag was to feel the impact in his home of two Balkan wars, dozens of revolutions, and the shot fired at Sarejevo, Bosnia, (now part of Yugoslavia) which assassinated the Archduke Francis Ferdinand

and triggered the long-lasting, terrible disaster of World War I. Battles, men, guns — yet his father spoke only of peace. Why were the other countries, and not Sweden, fighting? Dag didn't know. He only knew that it was a wonderful world when people did not have to leave their families and go off to shoot at each other.

On February 17, 1914, Hjalmar Hammarskjold was appointed, by royal decree, Prime Minister of Sweden, inheriting also the second crucial post of Minister of Defense.

"This was the start of three of the most demanding and controversial years of my entire life," Prime Minister Hammarskjold told his friends in later years.

It was predictable that he would have a hard time. The Prime Minister was leader of the Swedish government and of its wartime defense. He was pledged to maintain the neutrality of his country and to secure the betterment of its citizens. "Considering my own firm neutralist philosophies, and the state of world conflict, the contradictions of my office are overpowering," he told his wife.

The war years were a severe strain on Mrs. Hammarskjold, who worried constantly about her husband's arduous work. The plight of millions of soldiers and their loved ones saddened her to near depression at times. Prime Minister Hammarskjold's vigor, however, seemed to enlarge with his burdens. He even displayed more humor than usual, saying to her one cold winter morning as he left for an emergency conference:

[38]

"I have taken all precautions — I have even put on clean underwear." Agnes loved a touch of lightheartedness in her husband.

As a young teen-ager, Dag was tall for his age, with good features and a healthy ruddiness in his complexion. His sea-blue eyes, which seldom blinked, were his most striking feature. His worst feature was his nose; it was flat and a bit too broad at the tip, but it was inconspicuous in size. In all, he was considered handsome in a gentle sort of way. He was amazingly resistant to illness, and never suffered a serious ailment.

Dag resumed his friendship with Jon Olof Soderblom in the local high school they attended together. These two students soon made other friends, among them, Jarl Hjalmarson, the son of a colonel. Jarl felt more at ease with the prepossessing Jon than he did with Dag. Years later Jarl wrote the following about Dag:

"He was a nice chap but very reserved. We had respect for him, as one always does for one who is virtuous. Not that he was only studying . . . he was helpful and loyal . . . He was not considered boring or anything, but he had an indefinable don't-touch-me air that kept you at your distance. . ."

In the years after the war, when heads of state were trying to create a better world, there was a fever of activity in the heart of the university town of Uppsala. Hammarskjold, Soderblom, Schuck, Quense, Ribbing, Olivecrona - these names denoted the pillars of government and society, and there was a tight clannishness among these peo-

[39]

ple. The homes of these families were close together; it was virtually open house every day and night, and the families intermingled constantly. The sons and daughters of these noted figures got firsthand impressions of their elders' activities, and Dag was one of these lucky youths.

Bishop Soderblom had a considerable influence upon Dag, heightened by the fact that Dag's mother was a great friend of the Bishop. The clergyman and Mrs. Hammarskjold had been born on the same day, and were called "the twins" by friends. It was due to Bishop Soderblom's theological discussions that, in the summer of 1921, a year before graduating from high school, Dag decided to study religious philosophy with the famed minister, Bishop Carl Persson. A classmate, Yvonne Tengbom Wennerholm, who was preparing for her confirmation at the time, recalled this about Dag:

"The dialogue between Dag and Bishop Persson was on the highest intellectual level . . . I realized it was beyond my understanding as well as many of my friends. Dag was always more curious about challenging what Bishop Persson said, and then an animated exchange would take place . . ."

In social situations, Dag continued to be shy, but when it came to intellectual expression, he was not at all self-conscious or backward.

At eighteen, Dag's final high-school marks consisted of ten A's, including sketching; four A-minuses; and one B – in physical training.

[40]

When his father saw this report, he tried to say something which would keep his son from getting a swelled head:

"Aake's marks were better," Hjalmar Hammarskjold said clumsily, which wasn't quite true. Then, he decided to tell Dag how pleased he really was at his scholastic abilities. "If I had your brains," he joked, "I should have reached far."

Dag smiled appreciatively at his father's large compliment, and said, "Well, Papa, it's not so much my brains, but you who taught me 'how to get around the corner.'"

The senior Hammarskjold always used to tell his sons, "You have to get around the corner." In the Swedish idiom, it meant that one had to do things thoroughly and completely (getting around into the corners that were hard to reach).

Chapter 3

The Boy Makes the Man

Dag Hammarskjold was barely fourteen years old when World War I was drawing to a close. He was an impressionable youth who read a great deal and who heard much of the salon and table talk in his father's household.

Since Sweden was a neutral country, its people were the target of the propaganda from both the Allied nations and the Central Powers, as the German alliance was called. There were many conflicting viewpoints and exaggerated reports flowing into Stockholm in that dark era. Still there was perhaps more truth to be found in this country than others, because of its neutrality. The casualty lists, civilian and military alike, were poignant and unadorned.

The Allied blockade was creating hunger and deprivation in Germany, and Dag's father was often to be found in the midst of the Swedish effort to help feed the starving neighbor, Germany. Young Dag's mother was an active worker in several Swedish organizations engaged in aiding war victims.

So it was that the youngest Hammarskjold knew a lot about what was going on in the world around him. After observing so much misery in Europe, he saw the curtain go up on the Pyrrhic victory – its hopeful prologue, the "Fourteen Points" – and its disillusioning epilogue, the Treaty of Versailles. Although neither a "war baby" or a participating combatant (Dag's contemporaries in Germany were being sent to the front at 15), young Hammarskjold felt the impact of the events which were shaping the world into which he was maturing rapidly.

Even as a young boy, Dag had accustomed himself to enjoying the pleasures of solitary thinking. He had had to develop this inner resource because he had been left alone a good deal of the time.

Fortunately for him, he was born with a probing mind which made it possible for him to be alone and not be as lonely as others whose minds do not furnish them with "good company." This is one of the reasons Dag got on so well in his college studies at Uppsala University. He was more mentally and emotionally self-reliant than most young collegians. He could think for himself, and study in concentrated isolation without taxing himself. He studied literature, French, philosophy, and economics, absorbing these subjects with ease and deep interest. He even

[43]

found extra time to delve into unrequired subjects and to read widely. He mastered Spanish and Portugese. He was already fluent in German and Latin, and had learned English. Seven languages. Not bad for a youth barely out of his teens. He completed his university studies in two years.

The fact that Dag was the son of Sweden's top official who was often under partisan political attack in the press; that he lived in aristocratic surroundings in Vasa Castle, instead of a room on the University campus – these things were disadvantages. It was difficult enough for the circumspect Dag to broaden his friendships without having the added wall of "privileged aristocracy" around him. He was grateful for the friendship he continued to have with Jon Olof Soderblom, but there were some worthwhile fellows he would have liked to know better, but who kept their distance from him.

One young man who became one of Dag's closest friends was a medical student, Jan Waldenstrom. Dr. Waldenstrom remembers of that period:

"Dag used to look in at the college dining hall to try to catch our conversations, which were very lively. The philosophies of Freud and Hagerstrom and Spengler were the burning topics . . . Europe was another . . . Often, our differences of opinion would carry our talks far into the night, in our rooms, long after we'd left classes. It was during these unresolved debates that we would sometimes pick up Dag at Vasa Castle to get his fresh points We would take long walks with him and usually he would make us see things more clearly and solve the problems..."

It was clear to many young people in post-war "New Europe" that they were the "transient" generation, bridging an old world with the emerging new world. They realized fully the terrible price their fathers had paid for "victory" in World War I. They were asking the question: "Is it not possible that the world has learned its lesson? Is there nothing that can be done to see to it that no such crimes shall ever happen again? Is not all the suffering and destruction crushing indictment of the military epoch out of which no one has really emerged victorious?"

Dag Hammarskjold, coming into adulthood in those post-war years, found himself swept along by the dominating political current of the decade—the quest for peace, for disarmament. European boys acquire a political awareness very early in their 'teens, and this was especially true of young Dag, who lived in an intellectual climate both at home and at the university. There were occasions when he could ask the Prime Minister, his father, the meaning of a problem in international relations and receive an answer few other fathers could give.

Very early in life, Dag Hammarskjold developed to a fine art the trait of asking questions. To the occasional annoyance of many of his teachers, and of course his father and older brothers, he pursued his inquisitiveness with a quiet, but relentless, insistence on uncolored facts and absolute truth. He also possessed the trait of easily seeing through the facades with which people try to de-

[45]

ceive one another. He came to hold decided views about the statesmen who were actively shaping the treaties at Versailles and other post-war instruments. In the financial and economic settlements which affected Sweden more than the political pacts. Dag was impressed by the work of such men as John Maynard Keynes, whose *Economic Consequences of the Peace* became the standard textbook for students of the changing international order.

If, as has been said, "the boy makes the man," it was not too difficult in those days to discern that the tall, gangling student at Uppsala University was shaping his viewpoints and setting the mold for the casting of the adult Dag Hammarskjold. Like most youngsters, he had toyed with the notion of several careers. At fifteen he had decided, with a gesture of finality, to become a scientist. Nature, biology, the study of living things held his attention for a long time. Then came a time when literature, especially drama, excited him. He acted in a translation of a French play by Alfred de Musset. A Swedish publisher brought out a play written by young Hammarskjold. His friends in Stockholm bought copies, but the public showed no interest. His translations of the poetry of the future Nobel Prize winner St.-John Perse were on a different level, however. He was a great admirer of Perse, and did a most creditable job of interpreting the French poet.

Throughout his life, Hammarskjold retained his interest in poetry. He also loved strenuous physical activity. He became an avid and expert mountaineer, or Al-

Resting while climbing a mountain with a friend

pinist as the cognoscenti say. This dual concern with both
intellectual and physical activities squares with the philosophic view he held that every man had a need to see life
"steadily and see it whole," as Matthew Arnold expressed
it. He found this balance most important.

At another time in his student days he decided to be
a lawyer. After a few months of rest from his studies, he
entered Sigstuna College to take the course in jurispru-
dence.

He was not sure what his role in the future would be,
but he had decided that it would be in the economic, the
political, or the legal sphere. In Sweden, activity in these

fields invariably meant working with or for the state. His country was undergoing many changes as a consequence of the World War I and the peace settlements. Though it lived in "neutrality," Sweden did not live in "splendid isolation." It was being touched on all sides by violent boundary alterations and by the economic revolutions going on in neighboring countries. Sweden had its share of what today are called "angry young men." There were debates, arguments in the press, spirited elections, and the inevitable clashes between conservative and radical viewpoints.

A parliamentary reporter who had covered the Stockholm scene for more than a quarter of a century put it this way:

"When Dag Hammarskjold was at Uppsala, his country was undergoing a socialist orientation which was to bear fruit for the next two decades and bring about a condition as close to the welfare state as has been witnessed in any democratic nation in Europe. This meant that Hammarskjold has been serving socialist governments ever since he went into the civil service. Yet he never joined either the Socialist party nor the Conservatives [who brought his father to the premiership]. What he did was to walk a middle path, paying due heed to the democratic notion of a classless society while showing an aristocratic contempt for the idea of proletarian dictatorship."

He was not in agreement with much of the socialist philosophy, especially the pacifist internationalism of many of the leaders.

[48]

The great men of those days were busy determining the pattern of existence for almost everyone. But they were using the diplomacy of the past — power politics, secret agreements, and other outworn approaches. A northern European had a grandstand seat from which to watch the many conferences of Allied statesmen and the summit get-togethers of the Big Three, the Big Four, and the reparations squabblers. Dag Hammarskjold, like many others in neutral Sweden, believed that the old diplomatic habits would have to be abandoned, and that cooperation would have to be substituted for conflict in all international relations.

Along with many other young men of that time, Hammarskjold actively supported the League of Nations. Enthusiasm for the League was widespread in Europe — even in the neutral countries. There was the hope that the League would bring world peace out of the rosy distance of Utopia to the threshold of reality.

As a young man, Hammarskjold had a small taste of what it was like to take part in public affairs. When he was 22 years old, and still a student, he was appointed First Secretary of Uppland's 300th anniversary celebration. He had to take care of all arrangements, the thousand-and-one details which such an event involves. He made speeches, and to his surprise, he found that public exposure did not harm him after all. He forgot about himself, and he enjoyed the work.

Dag earned his law degree in 1930, spending his final year at Cambridge. His aim now was to get a job which would make use of his broad knowledge. His brilliance was no secret, but he was not expecting such good luck as being asked to become Secretary of the Unemployment Insurance Plan.

This plum, coming to Dag when he was only 25, was a great satisfaction to his father. The elder Hammarskjold's career had seen its height. He was no longer Prime Minister, and his vigorous policy-making days were over. He held many honorary posts — among them a lifetime membership in the Swedish Academy — and these kept him as busy as he wanted to be. But semi-retirement was upon Hjalmar Hammarskjold, and therefore it was no longer feasible or possible to stay on at Vasa Castle.

At a time when the family was saddened at parting from the home they'd known for 23 years, the news of Dag's appointment was a matter of immense pride to his father.

Agnes Hammarskjold's eyes were sparkling with the thought, "I told you so."

Sten, Aake and Bo congratulated their young brother with resounding slaps on the back.

Dag's own lightning career in government had begun.

Chapter 4

The Man Makes the Grade

E ven while he was merely an assistant professor of political economy at the University of Stockholm, Hammarskjold was astounding the nation's leading financial wizards with his grasp of complex fiscal problems. In 1933 he obtained his Ph.D. with a thesis carrying the jawbreaking title of *Konjunkturspridningen*, "A Theoretical and Historical Survey of Market Trends." It was a lengthy, involved, and vastly intricate work. It was also thoroughly dreary. Even the professors who graded doctorate papers found only one small touch of relief: a tongue-in-cheek preface in which Hammarskjold quoted the Duchess in *Alice in Wonderland:* "That's nothing to what I could say if I chose."

This frightfully complex work – practically impossible to translate into English – has since become something of a legend in Swedish academic circles. Some years after it was written, a fellow-economist named Jarl Hjalmarson — who subsequently became leader of Sweden's Conservative Party — planned to quote from the thesis in a debate on unemployment. Certain abstractions were beyond his grasp, and he decided to consult the author. Hammarskjold read the part in question several times, finally shook his head, and sheepishly confessed that he couldn't understand it either. When he had written the thesis he knew precisely what he had in mind, but apparently certain portions were too abstruse even for Hammarskjold's phenomenal memory.

Despite its dry-as-dust qualities, the thesis did more than produce yawns among the university faculty. Behind the complexity of the work, a brilliant mind was quite apparent. Hammarskjold not only earned his doctorate; he achieved almost overnight recognition among Sweden's top economic theorists. Shortly after he had finished the work, the 25-year-old assistant professor was approached by Ernst Wigforss, a former Minister of Finance and one of the nation's foremost monetary experts. Although Sweden had been isolated from war for 150 years, she was no less immune to world economic ailments than any other nation. All of Europe at that time was reeling under the impact of the world depression. Wigforss wanted Hammarskjold to head a committee being formed to combat Sweden's increasingly serious unemployment problem.

This was a considerable responsibility for a young

[52]

man whose experience up to then had been almost entirely theoretical. Nevertheless, Hammarskjold accepted the appointment with enthusiasm. After conducting an exhaustive survey of the unemployment picture, he set to work preparing a lengthy set of recommendations.

Like his thesis, the Hammarskjold unemployment report produced both a yawn and a gasp. Many of his colleagues on the committee had to read it several times over before they could get a proper picture from the voluminous mass of intricate detail that went into the work. But beneath the awesome layer of data lay a solid foundation of crystal-clear common sense. One writer summed up Hammarskjold's report this way: "It was bafflingly technical, but the practical measures he advocated kept unemployment lower in Sweden than in most European countries."

By now Hammarskjold had established himself solidly among the most prominent figures in the Swedish financial world. He consolidated this position as secretary of the Riksbank — the National Bank of Sweden - while simultaneously winning an international repute for articles published in the economic journals of other countries. Dull and unemotional as these works may have been - even to fellow experts long accustomed to tedious analysis and discourse — they nevertheless furnished further evidence of his unique grasp of the most bewildering fiscal refinements. It was no surprise to his colleagues when in 1936, at the age of 31. Dag Hammarskjold was made Permanent Secretary to the Ministry of

Finance. And it seemed no less fitting when he soon after became Chairman of the Riksbank, the first man ever to hold both posts at once.

A succession of brilliant strokes in office, a firm and well ordered administration, and a ledger all in the black proved that he was a clever civil servant, the right man for the right job. But there were very few clues to the statesman, the internationalist, tomorrow's Dag Hammarskjold.

Vilgot Hammarling, a member of the Swedish Foreign Office, once described Hammarskjold's career in government as similar to that of the "back-room boy" of British politics, the exceptionally gifted young man whose quiet, seldom-noticed efforts play a key role in formulating his country's policies. He became known as "the quiet young man who talked so little but did so much." When he was still in his thirties, he was acknowledged as Sweden's top monetary expert. At first, his work was directed chiefly at shaping the national budget structure, but later his responsibilities covered a much wider area.

In 1939, the unhealed wounds of World War I festered and broke out again in another global conflict. The Swedish government sent its "boy wonder" on many confidential and often dangerous diplomatic missions involving the delicate issue of his country's neutrality.

He moved about in the world's market places and procured much needed raw materials in competition with powerful buyers from the richer governments who

[54]

were competing in the arms race. Later he obtained radar and even jet aircraft for neutral Sweden's armed forces. Peace-maker Hammarskjold was an inconspicuous architect of Sweden's famed air arm which today ranks fourth among the world's air forces.

Many of the details of his early career may never be told. Hammarskjold left no memoirs as far as is known. He had an almost pathological distaste for "publicity," not only of the personal variety but also the official kind. Throughout his career Dag Hammarskjold was guided by the old maxim that silence is golden, and "if you can't be silent, be brief."

In pursuit of clues to the development of Hammarskjold the statesman, it should be recognized that in the decade preceding the outbreak of World War II his sole preoccupation was with money. Not the *making* of money, but with the role of money in a Europe teetering on the edge of war and social disintegration.

The peace of Versailles did not end the war of Dag's boyhood recollection; the war merely entered a new phase, waged by economic instead of military means. He witnessed the United States plunge into its worst depression. He had a close-up view of Germany seesawing between Communism and Nazism. Everywhere in Europe there was consternation over the fact that the United States was demanding the return of billions of dollars loaned to countries on the continent and to Britain. There were wild and serious threats of "cancellation" and "repudiation" from the creditor nations. Even

Sweden and Spain, non-combatants, did not escape the financial turmoil of that period.

Dag Hammarskjold found himself deeply enmeshed in his role of economic diplomat. In the early 30's he witnessed the resurgence of militarism all around him. His own country, an important producer of fine steel and munitions, participated in the re-arming of neighboring nations who were like actors in an impending drama, waiting in the wings for the curtain to rise.

Dag, the financial diplomat, was called to undertake heavier and heavier responsibilities. But these were very trying and difficult times for Dag, the peace-maker. His disillusionment was great as he saw the League of Nations grow weaker and weaker and finally dissolve at the outbreak of Hitler's war. But his faith in the idea behind the League was never shaken.

A fellow Scandinavian, Carl J. Hambro of Norway, who was the last president of the Assembly of the League of Nations, prophecied at the final session of the Assembly, "Our disappointments and disillusionments may be turned to use in cementing the structure of a new system of world security." Hammarskjold remembered this Scandinavian prophecy when he, himself, became part of the new "successful child of the League of Nations"—the United Nations.

At the end of World War II, Hammarskjold's horizons broadened. Transferred to the Foreign Office as under secretary in charge of financial affairs, he was largely responsible for reviving Sweden's overseas trade and securing vitally needed raw materials. On the domestic front, he played a leading role in staving off the threat of postwar inflation with a brilliant wage stabilization program. During the same period, his abilities began to win recognition among the nations which were later to sponsor his rise in the UN. At the Paris conferences of the Organization for European Economic Cooperation, all the delegates, and particularly the French, were astonished at Hammarskjold's capacity for work and his unerring ability to find the key to any difficult problem. "It is well known that very often when a document had to be drawn up and the delegates were faced with an evening of hard work, the job was left to Hammarskjold, who would be sure to know the subject back to front and what the point of view of the different delegates was," a colleague recalled.

The Paris conferees saw in Hammarskjold the high-level finesse of the gifted diplomat. It was inevitable that his public service career extend beyond the boundaries of economics. In 1951 he accepted appointment as Sweden's deputy foreign minister. From here, it was just a step to his country's delegation at the United Nations.

The brief history of the United Nations, prior to Hammarskjold's identification with it, was well known to him. He had watched his fellow Scandinavian, Trygve Lie, in his role as a controversial Secretary General and, no doubt, had his own views as to how the office should be conducted.

When and how did the United Nations originate?

In some respects, it can be called an outgrowth of the League of Nations, although there is no official or legal connection whatsoever between the two bodies. The League had failed tragically to achieve its principal goal of averting global conflict. Yet statesmen never lost sight of its lofty aims, even during the darkest days of World War II.

Indeed, as early as June 12, 1941, the representatives of five British Commonwealth nations and five Allied governments-in-exile reaffirmed their faith in the League's principles. The Inter-Allied Declaration, signed at St. James's Palace in London, stated: "The only true basis of enduring peace is the willing cooperation of free peoples. It is our intention to work together . . . both in war and peace, to this end."

Shortly after this, aboard a warship at a top-secret rendezvous "somewhere in the North Atlantic," the United States added the weight of its own endorsement to this moral alliance. President Franklin D. Roosevelt and Prime Minister Winston Churchill signed the historic Atlantic Charter. The idea that international cooperation had now become indispensable to world peace was embodied in the following words from this document: "After the final destruction of the Nazi tyranny, they hope to see established a peace which will afford assurance that all the men in all the lands may live out their lives in freedom from fear and want."

Belief in these principles grew progressively stronger during subsequent Allied conferences. The idea of a world organization to preserve peace was restated on January 1, 1942, in Washington, in a joint declaration of all nations fighting the Axis; on October 30, 1943, in Moscow, in a call for "a general international organization" by the United States, United Kingdom, Soviet Union and China; and on December 1, 1943, at Teheran, in a joint declaration by President Roosevelt, Prime Minister Churchill and Premier Stalin.

By 1944, when an Allied victory had become simply a matter of time, the idea of an international organization dedicated to world peace had crystallized to the point where active steps were taken. The first blueprint of the United Nations was drawn up at the Dumbarton Oaks Conference in Washington, during the summer and early autumn of that year. At this meeting, it was decided that the key body would be a Security Council, consisting of the "Big Five": The United States, Britain, France, the Soviet Union, and China. At the Yalta Conference on February 11, 1945, President Roosevelt, Prime Minister Churchill and Premier Stalin resolved that "a conference of United Nations should be called to meet at San Francisco . . . on the twenty-fifth of April, 1945, to prepare the charter of such an organization . . ."

San Francisco, then, can be called the birthplace of the United Nations. At this conference, the representatives of fifty nations met and drew up the Charter, the principles of which are:

1. To maintain international peace and security;

2. To develop friendly relations among nations based on respect for the equal rights and self-determination of peoples;

3. To cooperate in solving international problems of an economic, social, cultural or humanitarian character, and in promoting respect for human rights and fundamental freedoms for all;

4. To be a center for harmonizing the actions of nations in attaining these common ends.

On October 24, 1945, the Charter came into force when it was ratified by the "Big Five" of the Security Council and a majority of the other current members. October 24th is now observed as United Nations Day.

The three most important components of the United Nations are the Security Council, the General Assembly and the Secretariat. The Council consists of the so-called Big Five as permanent members, plus six non-permanent nations serving for two-year terms. Its principal responsibility is the maintenance of international peace and security. The Assembly consists of all member-nations, each with an equal vote. It has the right to discuss all matters within the scope of the Charter, and it prepares recommendations which all members are expected to accept, although the recommendations do not have the binding force of legislation. The Secretariat consists of the Secretary-General and his staff. The Secretary-General is the UN's chief administrative officers.

Since the Charter permits him "to bring to the at-

Getting advice from his predecessor, Trygve Lie, of Norway

tention of the Security Council any matter which in his opinion may threaten international peace," the Secretary-General's power and influence can be quite large, depending on how broad he interprets his power to be. Naturally Hammarskjold, in this situation, wielded enormous influence. In fact, it was on this article of the Charter that Dag based many of his actions for the maintenance of peace.

It was this inherent power, in fact, which brought about the downfall of Trygve Lie, the UN's first Secretary-General. From the very start, it was apparent that Russia wished to exercise far more power in the world organization than the Charter permitted to any single nation. It soon became apparent that the Soviet aim was to use the UN as an instrument for achieving its own ends. Under these conditions, a clash between Russia and the Secretary-General was inevitable. The clash eventually came about as the result of Lie's position on the Korean conflict. The Soviets forced Lie to resign on November 10, 1952.

Dag Hammarskjold was on a walking tour in Sweden when some reporters located him and told him that there was news from the UN in New York confirming the fact that he had been nominated by the French and endorsed by all the members of the Security Council for the job of Secretary-General. His answer to the press was a typical Hamarksjoldean retort, "Amused but not interested."

Months later, after he was in the job, he explained to intimates that when he was given the news by the reporters he thought that there had been some mistake in the report or that he was having his leg pulled. There were always a few jokesters around in Stockholm, and Dag suspected a hoax at his expense. His next communication was sent directly to New York. It was a more official query asking in effect, "What is this all about?" He had no idea at that time that he had just taken the first step toward becoming the new chief of the United Nations organization.

Chapter 5

New Broom in the Glass House

Shortly after he had been chosen by the General Assembly as the new Secretary-General, Dag Hammarskjold stepped into Trygve Lie's private elevator and zoomed to the 38th floor of the UN building. He was beginning a series of informal briefing sessions with the retiring incumbent. At their very first meeting, the blunt, stocky Lie told his successor, "The task for which you have been selected is absolutely impossible."

The quiet, sandy-haired Swede merely smiled.

What his inner emotions may have been one can only guess. He must certainly have been more than slightly surprised at finding himself chosen to guide the destinies of the United Nations.

When Dag Hammarskjold consented to enter the race for the position of Secretary-General, he was considered strictly a dark horse. The front-running candidates were Canada's Lester Pearson and several other well-known delegates. Most of the front-runners eventually appeared too controversial, but even so, Hammarskjold remained an outside choice. Scarcely anyone knew who he was or what he did, so quietly (and efficiently) had he functioned as one of Sweden's delegates to the world body. Trygve Lie had once described him as merely a "clerk," but at least the expansive Norwegian was aware of Hammarskjold's existence. That was something.

To the few who did know Hammarskjold, there could be no other choice. The French, very familiar with his work in the Swedish Ministry of Finance and Foreign Office, nominated him. The British approved the silent Scandinavian with the aristocratic background, impeccable manners and obvious instinct for impartiality and fair play. He was acceptable even to the Russians, who had been largely responsible for Lie's resignation, and whose "nyet" might well have been expected. But the Reds believed at the time that the candidate was "harmless." Valerian A. Zorin, Soviet Security Council delegate, even went so far as to say he would veto any name *but* that of Hammarskjold, a declaration the Soviets later pondered in anger. In any event, when the General Assembly voted, the results amounted to a Hammarskjold landslide.

Until 1953, Dag had been a relatively obscure Swedish economist and diplomat who went out of his way to avoid calling attention to himself. Now he suddenly found himself in the merciless glare of a never-ending barrage of flash bulbs, sharp questions from the press, and the searching lenses of television cameras. Shortly after taking office, he told a reporter: "What has happened to me is like being lifted by the scruff of the neck, as if I were a little dog, and being plunged into all those newsreels and flashbulbs. It's like a mirror suddenly held up before you in which you become distorted. It's like a very bad picture taken by a very bad photographer. I hope I shall survive."

He put it to the General Assembly more soberly: "Nobody, I think, can accept the position . . . knowing what it means, except from a sense of duty."

As the new Secretary-General saw it, his immediate task was to ignore the superficial clamor and get an understanding about his new job. Informal "kaffee klatches" with Lie were most helpful. And the outgoing Secretary-General quickly developed respect for his successor despite an undercurrent of antagonism.

"I admire Hammarskjold," he told a reporter one day. "I admire his intellect, his knowledge, and his administrative ability. I have left him many unsolved problems. I am not trying to tell him how to run the job. I did that once with someone many years ago in Norway, and it was the wrong thing. Hammarskjold comes in every afternoon for coffee — he will be coming in soon — and he asks questions. He must ask the questions, and then I will answer them. But he must find out for himself."

With Hammarskjold asking the right questions, the grim picture rapidly came into focus.

"It has been a terrible time," said Lie, soberly sum-

[65]

ming up. "After all, the Cold War started in 1946 – the year I became Secretary-General. We have had to struggle through crisis after crisis – in Palestine, in Iran, in Berlin, in Southeast Asia. We face what could become an insoluble problem in Korea, even though the end of the actual fighting may be in sight. But there are also many things for which we can be proud. We've brought some problems under control. Greece is quiet. So is Indonesia, although perhaps not as much as we might wish. Palestine has become Israel. We have these buildings; I always wanted the UN in New York, not so close to Europe. What we need is time . . . time. Just give us the time. That is what counts so much."

It was not necessary, of course, for Lie to recount his personal experiences. The former labor boss, always verbose and free with his opinions, had often put himself out on a fragile and dangerous limb. Unlike Hammarskjold, who practically never ventured personal comment on any nation's aims, Lie had frequently made his own views known. He had intervened publicly in delicate diplomatic matters concerning Spain, Iran, the question of seating Chinese Communists and, of course, Korea. The latter had proved to be his Waterloo. Although he had been almost conspicuous in trying not to antagonize Communist views by appearing to give open preference to the West, his career as Secretary-General foundered on the rocks of Joseph Stalin's fury in 1950, when he urged that the UN defend South Korea.

As a consequence of this action, the Russians vetoed

Lie's re-election when his first term expired that year. They went even further, making it known that they planned to exercise the veto over any other candidate put up by the West. The resulting deadlock produced a situation that seemed to call for a Philadelphia lawyer. It was finally resolved in a strange compromise. The Western powers, pointing out that the Charter did not specify any requirements or prohibitions on the temporary extension of a Secretary-General's term, proposed that Lie be accepted on this basis. Reluctantly — and surprisingly — the Soviets assented, and Lie's term was extended for three years. However, the U.S.S.R. continued its campaign to get rid of the Secretary-General by the simple device of refusing to recognize his existence. Communications from the Soviet delegation were sent to the Secretariat as a body, but not to Lie. Inevitably, this situation became intolerable.

Later, in memoirs entitled '*In The Cause of Peace*,' Lie wrote: "The influence of the United Nations for peace was weakened when its Secretary-General could not exercise . . . his office as the universally recognized spokesman for the whole organization . . . I desired that my continued presence . . . should not reduce . . . the chance of preventing war and preserving peace. "Under the conditions which the Russians had artificially created, Lie felt that it would be impossible for the UN to function effectively. It took rare strength of character to admit defeat, but in resigning, Lie did just that.

[67]

Since the time of Lie's resignation, the situation has changed. Admission of many small nations has obliterated the vote majority formerly held by the major powers — at least in the General Assembly. Hammarskjold was able to use this weapon against Soviet demands that he follow his predecessor's example and resign. But when he first took office, he was every bit as vulnerable as the burly Norwegian who had just been forced out.

The "kaffee klatches" lasted only as long as they served a purpose, for Dag was anxious to roll up his sleeves. He began right in the UN building itself, where morale was low. He knew that no leader could function better than the team with which he must work, and he resolved to talk informally to "his people."

He explained to his then executive assistant, Andrew Cordier, an ex-professor from Indiana, that he wished to meet every U. N. employe in the entire builidng, from department heads to the most insignificant stenographer. And, he added, he wanted to meet each of them personally. Cordier performed a hasty exercise in mental arithmetic.

"But that will take at least two months, Mr. Secretary."

Hammarskjold's blue eyes crinkled in a smile. "No it won't," he replied quietly, and added, "I believe we ought to approach this floor by floor. I should like to begin today."

That is precisely what he did, shaking hands with

every one of the four thousand UN employes in the building. "I am here," he would say on entering each department, "to serve you all." In effect, he told the entire staff that they were not working for him, but that all — including himself — were working together. This unique

Talking with his under-secretary, Dr. Ralph Bunche

feat in employer-employe relations was finished at the end of fourteen days. And Dag Hammarskjold had four thousand new, loyal friends.

The handshaking tour was no grandstand gesture, but the sincere effort of a leader to unify his subordinates. This effort was evident in a variety of other ways, too. Although Hammarskjold may have valued his personal privacy above anything else, he knew that privacy must not extend to the United Nations, which by its very nature is public property. Accordingly, one of his first acts as Secretary-General was to give orders that the private elevator, the one on which he had ridden for his first meeting with Trygve Lie, be operated for the service of the entire Secretariat staff. Not long after that, in the UN employes' cafeteria, a filing clerk happened to notice a quiet, sandy-haired man standing behind him holding a tray. The clerk gulped, and offered his place to the Secretary-General. Hammarskjold gestured him back with a gentle smile. For a while, the spectacle of the UN's top man on the "chow line" was fairly common. But more often he held informal lunch conferences in the delegate's restaurant, sharing a window table with his two assistants, Andrew Cordier and Ralph Bunche. (However, after the Congo crisis began in 1960, it became more difficult for him to take time away from the 38th-floor office.)

These modest habits reflected Dag's instinct for practical democracy. They also revealed a frugality that became even more apparent in his early efforts at cutting Secretariat expenses. Trimming an already skin-tight budget proved to be a monumental task, and many an economic wizard might have quailed at the complexities of balancing Secretariat books. However, to the man who had almost single-handedly ended Sweden's unemployment problem during the depression, it was simply a matter of applying knowledge and common sense. Within weeks of assuming his new post, he had sliced the Secretariat budget by one million dollars.

When plans were being made to celebrate the UN's tenth anniversary in San Francisco, a staff member asked the Secretary-General which officials should fly to the coast first class, and which should fly tourist. Hammarskjold looked up, mildly surprised that the question should even arise.

"Everyone will fly tourist, of course," he said. He made it plain that "everyone" included the Secretary-General.

Hammarskjold's insistence on lopping every superfluous expense was reflected in countries around the-world. A classic example of the power of his influence occurred in the tiny West African republic of Togo (formerly French Togoland). The country's premier, Sylvanus Olympio, had graduated from the London School of Economics and had always been impressed by Hammarskjold's financial accomplishments. One of Olympio's first goals in his new office was to wipe out a national deficit by strict enforcement of tax laws and careful auditing of government accounts. In this task he did not spare even himself. Instead of emulating the high brass of other nations by giving himself a shiny limousine with chauffeur, the new prime minister set a national example by riding to his office every morning on a bicycle. He also called attention to his firm guardianship of Togo's

[71]

funds by turning off his refrigerator every night before he went to bed.

"I wouldn't want the electric people to think I'm being extravagant," he explained.

If Hammarskjold had limited his responsibilities merely to handshaking and budget-trimming, he could have had an orderly and pleasant career as Secretary-General. This, of course, he could not do. He knew that he must lose no time in re-establishing the prestige of his office which the Soviets had so recklessly weakened. This would unquestionably put him on the wrong side of the Soviet delegation which had regarded him as "harmless," but the Secretary-General had never been concerned about his personal popularity.

Curiously enough, the first nation which he antagonized was not Russia but the United States. One of his earliest acts in the Cold War was to press for early settlement of the Korean conflict. This required a good deal of determination and courage. Although most free world nations sent contingents to serve under the blue UN flag, the vast majority of the UN army consisted of United States ground, sea and air forces, and the entire Korean campaign was to all practical purposes a U.S. operation. Moreover, American sentiment was overwhelmingly in favor of a decisive military victory. Thus, Hammarskjold's debut on the international powder keg was tantamount to opposing the United States. Calling for "peace without vengeance," he urged that the UN command in Korea forego the conventional military triumph.

"In the light of this international action," he said, "inherited notions will have to be abandoned. Although [a negotiated cease-fire] may not be considered as satisfactory by those who still believe in the unconditional surrenders of old wars, [it] is a full vindication of those brave men who have sacrificed their lives for this principle."

In effect, Hammarskjold was introducing practical application of the Golden Rule to a 20th Century war that threatened to spread beyond control. He was proclaiming to the UN members with forces in Korea that two wrongs simply do not make a right.

The Korean armistice was signed on July 27, 1953.

Delegates now began to recognize the formerly obscure Swedish economist as the UN's "spokesman for civilization." Yet it became obvious that he was considerably more than a starry-eyed idealist with no regard for practical realities. When he said, "To the diplomat of the 20th Century, war is something that must be averted at almost any cost," member-nations took note of that key word "almost." Hammarskjold realized that armed conflict, unspeakable as it may be, is not necessarily going to vanish from the face of the earth just because it happens to be unpopular.

In his first annual report to the General Assembly, Dag insisted, with unusual candor, that member-nations stop using the UN as a sounding board for all their troubles. There is a great deal more to the task of achieving world peace, he said, than simply complaining. "Come up with constructive suggestions," he told the delegates, "not merely charges against other nations."

Years before, Dag's family had been surprised by his switch from the profession of teacher to that of financial expert. But in fact, he never stopped being a teacher, even in the United Nations. With the world body, his lessons covered a far wider range than economics. Hammarskjold's new class was now composed of delegates from nearly a hundred nations. His principal subject concerned the reconciliation of differences —"harmonizing" was his favorite expression. And like the teacher who must occasionally separate two small boys from a classroom free-for-all, Hammarskjold was keeping apart the armed might of scores of sovereign nations.

He knew that every element of his training, every ounce of his instinct, would be only barely sufficient for the unimaginable task that faced him. Yet there was never a question in his mind as to his own survival, for the personal philosophy which guided him throughout his long public career was one of tough, realistic optimism. He never minimized the gravity or difficulty of a problem, yet he was totally unable to regard a job as impossible.

In an address at Cambridge University, Dag referred to the awful potential unleashed by scientific advances in nuclear physics. He went on, however, to underline its unlimited possibilities to improve man's

[74]

lot in the world.

". . . The peaceful use of atomic energy holds promise, too, that problems such as those posed by the world's population explosion, for example, may well also be solved through this modern energy," he said. Admitting that the goal of total disarmament was still far off, he nevertheless declared emphatically: "Note, however, the gains in international cooperation in the peaceful uses of atomic energy . . . We have installed world-recognized safety measures, we have promoted wide exchange of scientific information. This is a very good beginning."

Such stubborn optimism was perhaps an outgrowth of Hammarskjold's wide experience as an expert mountain climber. Indeed, he often likened his UN talk to the dangerous business of scaling a challenging peak.

"The safest climber," he once said, "is he who never questions his ability to overcome the next difficulty." Elaborating, he went on to stress the mountaineer's need for "perserverance, patience and a firm grip on realities, careful but imaginative planning, a clear awareness of the dangers, but also of the fact that fate is what we make it."

Hammarskjold apparently considered that it was necessary for him to create an evasive facade. One time in the UN Delegates' Restaurant—perhaps the world's most cosmopolitan eating place—an Arab delegate was discussing the Secretary-General with a colleague.

"Mr. Hammarskjold," he said, "often brings to mind the old fable of the Eastern merchant who was sending his son into the world to seek his fortune. He said to the young man, 'There are two precepts I would have you remember at all times. The first is to keep your promises, whenever you have made them, whatever they may be.'

"The son nodded and said, 'Yes, father. And what is the second?'

"To this, the merchant replied, 'Never make any promises.'"

Sly, non-commital elusiveness was by no means the personal monoply of Dag Hammarskjold. Every diplomat has to make use of it when the situation demands. Yet Hammarskjold may well have brought the practice to a degree of perfection never before attained in the history of international relations.

His evasiveness was a factor in his rather cool relations — to put it mildly — with the press. When he took office, reporters assigned to the UN had long been accustomed to the colorful and talkative Trygve Lie, whose grandiose pronouncements were always "hot copy." Dag was mute by comparison. Unlike his predecessor, who relished the opportunity of offering his personal opinion on any subject, Hammarskjold rigidly kept his own views to himself. His statements to the press were often deliberately ambiguous. Such an attitude can be infuriating to men who must rely on straight-forward answers to straight-forward questions, and UN correspondents constantly complained about Hammarskjold's diplomatic double-talk in press conferences.

Worse, Hammarskjold never concealed his distaste for the Fourth Estate. In spite of this, reporters on the UN beat went out of their way to be fair and even generous to Hammarskjold. Normally, no such courtesy is shown to anyone so thoroughly uncooperative. But although correspondents raged at the scarcity of headline copy to be squeezed from the Secretary-General, they themselves recognized the necessity for evasiveness in his delicate position.

Hammarskjold's elusive personality was countered by his refined manner. His soft-spoken courtesy is a far cry from the brawling, extroverted Lie, who came up the hard way, through the violent, two-fisted roughand-tumble of trade-union politics. Yet it is a mistake to think that Dag was a less rugged individual.

The Secretary-General indeed often showed that he could be very tough, especially when the principles of the United Nations were at stake. In the spring of 1961 he was under the heaviest fire he had ever experienced as UN chief. The Russians, infuriated by two successive failures to have their way in the Congo, were now stepping up the pace of their campaign to remove Hammarskjold from office. The personal aspect of the attack scarcely disturbed him. His concern was over the Soviet proposal that the entire office of Secretary-General be abolished, and replaced by a three-man "troika" commission consisting of representatives of the East, West, and neutral nations. This plan, Hammarskjold knew, would only weaken the United Nations, and remove forever its power to keep the nations of the world from one another's throats. He stressed this fact in a speech at Oxford University.

"World peace may be endangered," he said, "if the United Nations rejects the principle of an international secretariat directed by a truly independent chief executive." The members of the proposed "troika" group, he pointed out, "obviously would not be supposed to work in the direction of an internationalism considered unpalatable to their governments . . .

"To abandon or to compromise with principles on which such cooperation is built," he concluded, "may be no less dangerous than to compromise with principles regarding the rights of a nations. In both cases, the price to be paid may be peace."

Dag Hammarskjold was informing the world that it faced the choice of abandoning an admittedly imperfect international arbitration machine for an apparatus which would almost certainly destroy the UN as an instrument of peace.

Furious assaults were launched at Hammarskjold whenever a particular nation did not like the Secretary-General's stand on an issue. The Russians called him "a lackey of the imperialists" because of his firm insistence on peace in the Congo. The United States was sharply critical of his failure to place the blame more squarely on Russia when Red troops moved into Hungary.

Britain and France became furious when he forced the end of their lightning Suez campaign. France went so far as to conduct a calculated program of high-level snobbery against the Secretary-General, culminating in a refusal to receive him in Paris during the Bizerte crisis. South Africa extended a similar rebuff after the Sharpeville massacre in 1960, arguing that a visit by the Secretary-General would constitute meddling in an "internal affair."

But after these ruffled tempers subsided and the counsel of reason returned, there always emerged an unqualified respect for Hammarskjold. The South African government ultimately relented and offered him a formal invitation. Britain and France gave him staunch support in disputes even when his expressed views opposed their own foreign policies. And no member-nation stood behind Hammarskjold more consistently than the United States. Even the Russians, on occasion, acknowledged his unique qualifications as arbiter of the world's roughest game.

The Secretary-General's respect for others could also be seen in his high degree of sensitivity to personal considerations. For instance, although he was known as a stickler for business-like efficiency in all aspects of his work, Hammarskjold never used the office buzzer when he wanted to summon one of his two top aides. Instead, he left his desk and walked into their offices. He considered buzzers cold, impersonal, and ill-mannered.

He once expressed his unswerving belief in human dignity by the following words, "Whatever political system you have, it must be based on respect for the individual." He never allowed himself to forget the importance of the individual man as a *human being*, even when that human being was pounding his shoe on a desk in an offensive personal diatribe against him.

Hammarskjold realized that a nation can often be as sensitive as a person, particularly a newly independent, underdeveloped country that is striving for acceptance. For this reason, he emphasized the need for assisting such nations with the same kind of understanding one would extend to a fellow man. He pointed out that the United Nations Special Fund, which provides technical assistance and financial investment, is the ideal instrument to aid "have-not" nations without offending their national pride.

"You realize," he once said, "that it is sometimes more difficult to receive than to give . . . Under a multilateral system, in a world where we all share our common fate, it reflects on no one's dignity when aid is proferred or accepted."

He was a firm believer in what has been described as "personal diplomacy." Between 1953, and his death in 1961, Hammarskjold made one-man missions to nearly every member-nation of the UN, traveling nearly a million miles in the process. He tramped the hot sands of the Negev Desert in long walks with Israeli premier Ben-Gurion discussing Greek philosophy and Hassidic mysticism. He sipped cup after cup of syrupy coffee in lengthy private conferences with Nasser in Cairo. He went rowing on the choppy Black Sea with Khrushchev. Even non-UN members played host to Dag. During his mission to negotiate for the freedom of the American

Flying home after spending Christmas with UN troops in Gaza

airmen in Red China, he dined on bird's nest soup and rotten eggs with Premier Chou En-lai.

There was nothing dramatic or flamboyant about Hammarskjold's drop-of-the hat trips to the four corners of the earth. Dag merely made reservations for a seat

[81]

on a commercial airline, or he took a military transport plane. He put in a surprise appearance in the desert during the Suez crisis, disembarking with the first detachment of troops of the UN Emergency Force. In Europe—particularly during vacations—he often traveled second class and, with a minimum of official underlings.

No bands played, no salutes were fired, no speeches were made when the Secretary-General arrived in a city. Occasionally, he was greeted in a manner decidedly not friendly. During the Bizerte crisis, he was stopped by a French sentry outside the Tunisian city and ordered to get out of his car so it could be searched. Even after Hammarskjold identified himself as the UN Secretary-General, the rude inspection continued. Dag did not take this affront personally as other men might have. While on United Nations business, he was indifferent to everything but the fact that he had a job to do.

Hammarskjold was ready, willing, and conspicuously able to take personal command of any tough situation. If air travel wasn't fast enough, he used the telephone. When he had to muster troops to avert bloody chaos after the Congolese Army mutinied in 1960, he simply rang up a dozen African prime ministers and presidents and told them what must be done. The first armed troops were debarking from transport planes in Leopoldville and Stanleyville only 48 hours later.

"I believe that it is in keeping with the philosophy of the Charter," he said during the debate on Suez, "that the Secretary-General should be expected to act

. . . in order to help in filling any vacuum that may appear in the systems which the Charter and traditional diplomacy provide for the safeguarding of peace and security."

Allied with his belief in direct, forceful personal action, was his practice of what reporters have dubbed "quiet diplomacy." The age-old comparison with the iceberg – one-eighth visible, the remainder beneath the surface – is helpful in understanding deliberations. Open meetings of the Security Council and General Assembly constitute only a small fraction of vital UN business. Many of the UN actions that produced headlines began in closed-door sessions, in drawn-out, give-and-take bargaining discussions in committee rooms. The tireless Secretary-General was the ideal personality to guide the progress of these behind-the-scenes conferences. It was sometimes said that he was like a little boy who spoke only when spoken to. While this is far from being entirely true, his soft-spoken diplomatic know-how had a way of bringing order and accomplishment from chaotic disagreement. When he emerged from his countless "under-water" sessions, he knew almost to a word, what the various speakers would say in the Council and the Assembly.

What trait was most dominant in the Secretary-General? There are many opinions. Some delegates, like the Arabs, were impressed with his evasive sleight-of-hand diplomacy. Others respected his impartiality or his reliability in times of crisis. He was many things to many people. Those with whom Hammarskjold worked most closely gained an inspiration from his unshakable dedication to the UN goal. For despite his consideration for others, his never-failing courtesy and all the urbane characteristics of the cultivated gentleman he was still the man who said:

"A mature man is his own judge. In the end, his only firm support is being faithful to his own convictions. The advice of others may be welcome and valuable, but they do not free him from responsibility . . .

"Descending from generations of soldiers and government officials on my father's side I have inherited the opinion that nothing could be more satisfactory in life than unselfishly to serve your country - or humanity. This means that you have to sacrifice all personal interests, and also that you have to have the courage to stick to your opinions in the face of all opposition."

Chapter **6**

From Peiping to Geneva

United Nations press headquarters were more crowded than usual. Reporters talked anxiously in small groups. Photographers and newsreel cameramen re-checked their equipment. A telephone jangled and a reporter seized the receiver. ". . . No, not yet. Any minute now. I'll get it to you just as soon as it breaks."

Outside, a chill, slashing rain obscured the view of the East River. But no one noticed the weather. All eyes were on the door to the big press room, as nearly a hundred correspondents waited for Dag Hammarskjold to enter.

On that raw December afternoon in 1954, Henry Cabot Lodge, United States Ambassador to the United Nations, had asked for an all-out UN effort to free some two dozen U.S. Air Force flyers who had been captured by Chinese Communist troops during the Korean conflict. The Lodge resolution had called on Dag Hammarskjold to use his personal influence, his own "good offices." The General Assembly had passed the resolution.

To the press, this could mean only one thing. Hammarskjold would have to visit Red China himself, since that nation was not a member of the UN. No sooner had Hammarskjold entered the room, his blue eyes squinting slightly in the blinding glare of flashbulbs and television floodlights, than the question was put to him directly.

"Mr. Secretary, considering the outcome of the vote on the Lodge resolution, do you plan to consult personally with the Red Chinese government in Peiping?"

Although he hesitated before answering Hammarskjold was not at all surprised by the question. Smiling, he replied, "Wouldn't that be rather dramatic?"

Of all the evasive answers which the Secretary-General had given to the press during his first year in office, this must have been the most exasperating. Yet he had chosen deliberately to be noncommittal; a "dramatic" gesture may well have been worst possible action he could have taken.

The American flyers had been imprisoned for several years. The charges of "spying" brought against them were flimsy justification for a savage violation of international law. Even after the cease-fire and end of hostilities on the Korean front, the Peiping government had declared its intention of holding the Americans indefinitely. The Chinese Communists had no right to hold these men prisoner. They seemed to be doing it as a gesture of raw belligerence, as if to say, "What are you going to do about it?"

The problem of dealing with the Chinese was ex-

Dag meets Premier Chou En-lai of Red China

tremely touchy. A great deal of antagonism against Red China existed in the United States. Many members of Congress had demanded direct action to secure the prisoners' release. They were calling for a blockade of Red Chinese ports by the U. S. Seventh Fleet, and other actions. Popular sentiment was highly emotional.

Relations between Hammarskjold and Lodge were little better than cordial. Yet Lodge was virtually putting his prestige into the Secretary-General's hands in proposing personal action by Hammarskjold. Temperamentally and politically Lodge and Hammarskjold were opposites. Perhaps their only common ground in 1954 was their mutual faith in the potential of the UN as an international intermediary.

But even this presented a problem, for too much support from Lodge could endanger the UN mission. The United States, had consistently opposed Red China's admission to the UN. Many of Hammarskjold's colleagues in the Secretariat felt that UN intervention threatened to bring the world body perilously close to playing a part in American politics. They urged the Secretary-General not to make a trip to Red China. The United States, they felt, had handed their chief a genuinely hot potato.

The Secretary-General listened courteously—and very attentively—to the many valid points raised against his contemplated one-man mission. But he made no comment. Then, one morning he phoned his Park Avenue apartment and asked for Bill Ranallo, his personal aide.

"Bill," he said, "will you please pack one suitcase for me? Pack your own, too, and be sure you have a heavy overcoat. Will you also get airline tickets for Peiping? Tourist, of course. Oh, and pack my camera."

[88]

Then, reluctantly, he called a press conference and announced his decision. This time, the press got a straight news story from the Secretary-General, with no diplomatic evasions.

"This will be spectacular, Mr. Secretary!" declared a reporter.

"Too spectacular, perhaps," replied Hammarskjold grimly.

As the big DC-7C droned over the Pacific, Hammarskjold must have wondered what kind of reception awaited him in Peiping. Despite the formal politeness of the Red Chinese reply to his request for a personal conference, he had no way of knowing what the reaction to his proposal would be. Despite his years of travel, he had never before visited the Far East. Nor had he ever met Red China's handsome, cold-eyed Premier Chou En-lai.

He was well aware of some of the enormous obstacles facing him. Even if Red China were a less stubborn nation, there was the problem—incomprehensible to the West—of "face." Among Eastern leaders from Manchuria to Malaya, this intangible had long dominated their thinking. "Face" would have been a colossal roadblock even if the Chinese Communists were favorably disposed toward freeing the American flyers. And they were emphatically—and adamantly—nothing of the sort.

As if all this were not enough, Hammarskjold also realized how easily Red China's propaganda machine could exploit the charge that he was acting as a "puppet" of the United States government. And as Secretary-General of the United Nations, he might automatically be *persona non grata* in Red China. After all, it was under the blue flag of the UN that Red China's military might had been held at bay in Korea.

Nearly the only bright spot in the picture was Hammarskjold's knowledge that it was his predecessor, Trygve Lie, and not himself, who had supported the UN action against the Chinese Communists. There was also a potential ace in the hole. The Red Chinese government entertained high hopes of eventual admission as a member of the United Nations; it would not be likely to show any desire or intention of alienating the Secretary-General of that body.

Hammarskjold and a handful of aides got off the plane at Peiping's airport on a bitterly cold morning in January, 1955. There is perhaps no other metropolis on the face of the earth that has the hypnotic charm of this city. Its towering rock walls have stood massively withdrawn from centuries of invasions and revolutions. In this seat of numberless ancient dynasties and empires, there is a feeling of philosophic, timeless calm. Few are not caught in its spell. Indeed, it may be that the only people unaffected by Peiping's rich oriental heritage are the Red Chinese themselves.

Nevertheless, the Communist leaders, from Chou on down, received Hammarskjold at their capital with precise and impeccable Eastern courtesy. No gesture

William Ranallo (left) accompanies Dag to Red China

of respect was overlooked. Hammarskjold was given spacious quarters in Chou's own residence. He was taken on tours of the city. Red China's new factories are its proudest showcases; Hammarskjold must have had to exercise his tact to the utmost on seeing the appalling working conditions under which the "New China" was being built.

His hosts treated him to rare oriental delicacies at meals, and were surprised at his skill in wielding the unfamiliar chopsticks. All in all, the Secretary-

[*91*]

General was given a full-scale "red carpet" treatment. A European businessman who was in Peiping at the time reported that Hammarskjold's reception was far more elaborate than the welcomes usually accorded him in other world capitals. "The only thing missing," he said, "was personal warmth."

When all the ritual of greeting ended, Hammarskjold and Chou went into a locked-door conference. It was a strange meeting. There had been no precedent for such talks in the UN's history; the idea of the Secretary-General sitting down with the leader of a non-member government in an effort to help the imprisoned citizens of that non-member's bitterest enemy might have been unthinkable only a few months previously. There was also a distinct air of secrecy about the Hammarskjold mission. No reporters had been permitted to accompany the small UN delegations.

Despite the top-secret atmosphere of the meeting, there is no question that Hammarskjold relied heavily on his new status as "World Citizen Number One." He counted, optimistically, on his role as an impartial "servant" whose duty was to uphold and further the principles of the UN Charter. In this role he hoped to effect a partial thaw in the frigid courtesy of the Communist Chinese. In talking with Chou and his advisers, he emphasized that as "Mr. UN", he represented *all* member governments, not merely the nation directly concerned. He further pointed out, "I am spokeman not only for the non Communist states, but for Communist members as well."

[92]

Chou certainly could deny none of this, especially at a time when the Russians were still on fairly good terms with Hammarskjold, and also at a time when differences between Chinese and Soviet Marxists had yet to produce a major rift between the two Red behemoths. Chou finally told Hammarsjold, "I will seriously consider your request."

There was another flurry of protocol as the Secretary-General thanked the Red Chinese for his courteous reception. Then the tiny party returned to New York. On the plane, Hammarskjold was less talkative than ever. Aside from taking a few hours of badly needed sleep, he spent the entire trip reading a Proust novel. Even the aides who accompanied him had no idea what his thoughts were.

Events during the following months were anything but encouraging. Shortly after Hammarskjold's return from Peiping, an Indian transport plane, which was to have carried Chou to an Asian conference, exploded in flight. Only a last-minute decision to take another aircraft had saved the Red Chinese premier from certain death. It was subsequently learned that a Nationalist Chinese agent, posing as a maintenance worker, had planted a bomb in the plane as it was being serviced.

Nor were Red Chinese attitudes softened by the alerting of the Seventh Fleet when Communist artillery opened up on the offshore islands of Quemoy and Matsu. It was a time to try the confidence of even the sturdiest mountaineer. As the months went by with no word from Peiping, the general feeling in the Secretariat—and in Washington—was that Hammarskjold's mission had been a failure.

Yet the Secretary-General gave no indication that he had lost hope. Work in the 38th floor office continued at its usual relentless pace, for Hammarskjold was now deeply involved in a project that would have every bit as much effect on the future of the United Nations as his apparently unsuccessful attempt to free the U. S. flyers. And once again, Hammarskjold found himself the man in the middle, facing the seemingly impossible task of preparing a meeting-ground for two diametrically opposed ideologies.

The project had its beginning shortly after President Eisenhower's 1953 inauguration. At that time, one of the new President's chief concerns was the growing atmosphere of world despair that had begun with the dropping of the first atom bomb on Hiroshima. The unspeakable horrors of a possible all-out nuclear war had taken hold of the morbid side of the man's imagination. President Eisenhower felt that his wave of apprehension, while understandable, was shortsighted. As he saw it, the world was frantically concerned with the destructive power of the atom, and in the process was overlooking its limitless potential benefits. Even the mushroom cloud of gloom hanging over the world, he thought, could have its own silver lining.

Late in 1953, Ambassador Lodge felt it might be

well for the President to address the UN General Assembly. Mr. Eisenhower, in turn, considered this the proper forum in which to discuss the peaceful uses of atomic energy. On December 8, 1953, the representatives of 60 nations crowded the great hall on the East River, to listen to the man who had been Supreme Allied Commander in World War II.

"It is not enough to take this weapon out of the hands of soldiers," said Eisenhower. "It must be put into the hands of those who will know how to strip its military casing and adapt it to the arts of peace . . ." As his speech progressed, he proposed the formation of an atomic energy agency within the framework of the United Nations.

At first, this idea did not seem startling to the delegates. An atomic energy body was nothing new in itself; all nations with nuclear weapons had their own such agencies. However, the meaning of Eisenhower's speech finally took hold. His suggestion to place closely guarded secrets — which had produced the atomic and hydrogen bombs — at the disposal of the entire world for the purpose of securing peace was a unique opportunity

Even so, despite the new note of hope which Eisenhower had introduced to the world scene, the Soviets were unmoved. They merely repeated their well-worn argument that nothing could be done about atoms for peace until and unless the Western powers agreed to outlaw atoms for war. In the face of this resistance, Eisenhower nevertheless remained convinced that East and West could meet.

And meet they did. Between mid-January and mid-September of 1954, private talks were held between representatives of the U.S.S.R. and U.S.A. A detailed blueprint for an atomic energy agency linked to the United Nations began to take shape following a series of meetings between Secretary of State John Foster Dulles and Soviet Foreign Minister V. M. Molotov. At first, prospects for real cooperation seemed bright. However, it presently became evident that Russia was not going to budge from her original position, and the ambitious plans threatened to become just another scrap of paper. Accordingly, when the ninth session of the UN General Assembly gathered in New York that fall, the U. S. government acted almost in desperation. Exercising its privilege, it referred the atoms-for-peace matter back to the Assembly.

A year had elapsed since President Eisenhower's speech. The General Assembly now put the matter directly into Hammarskjold's hands. In a resolution, adopted unanimously in December 1954, he was instructed to arrange the first International Conference on the Peaceful Uses of Atomic Energy. The concept of this meeting had emerged from an idea—originally propounded in the United States—which envisaged the ultimate creation of an international atomic energy agency. Whether or not such a group would develop from the conference was not known. However, it was hoped at the very least that the meeting would be a first step toward giving atoms-for-peace a high priority in the UN order of business. That it proved to be.

Hammarskjold acted swiftly. To provide top executive authority that would expedite arrangements for the conference, he appointed Dr. Ralph Bunche as his chief assistant. Bunche, who had already proved himself to be a brilliant organizer and negotiator, would in turn be assisted by Dr. Gunnar Randers of Sweden and Ilya S. Tcherychev of the Soviet Union. The formation of this team would not only facilitate preparations for the meeting, it would also give Hammarskjold himself more opportunity to guide the entire project. And his guidance was vital to the outcome of the conference, as he knew it could succeed only if the participating nations—particularly the United States and Russia—kept it entirely free of cold war politics.

This very problem was presented to him by an aide who had been working on some of the routine details of the conference.

"I don't want to seem skeptical, Mr. Secretary," he said. "But can we really expect any significant developments from this meeting? After all, the delegates are going to represent countries that don't trust each other on the simplest diplomatic procedures. Just how realistic is it to assume that they'll suddenly start giving away their top-secret nuclear information? Look at the five-nation meetings between the United States and Russia. They just broke up with nothing accomplished. Why do we have any reason to believe that we can handle this any more effectively?"

"Perhaps we can't," replied the Secretary-General. "But it must be remembered that there is a difference. This is a United Nations conference, and we can hope that it will create a climate of mutual trust where other meetings have not. I have to assume that scientists can do the one thing that terrifies a politician: ignore the traditional barriers of ideology that have always kept nations apart and suspicious. If my assumption is wrong. . ." He shrugged his shoulders and added quickly, "But I don't think it will be."

It was soon proved that Hammarskjold had reasoned correctly. The preliminary meeting were held in Paris in May, 1955, attended by some of the most brilliant scientific minds in the history of the world. Both the U. S. and U.S.S.R. sent their best men. The chief Russian scientist was nuclear expert D. V. Skobeltzin; Nobel Prize winner I. I. Rabi of Columbia University headed the American delegation. But the real star of the performance was not even a scientist. Under Dag Hammarskjold's tactful chairmanship, the nuclear group worked more smoothly and effectively than had any previous East-West conference under UN auspices. There was not a single detail in the entire program to which he did not give his careful attention — and for which he did not take personal responsibility. Even the seating arrangements for lunches and dinners at Geneva's attractive Restaurant du Lac came under his protocol-trained scrutiny. But because of the very fact that the deliberations produced no wrangling, they received practically no publicity – once again proving the newspaperman's old adage that disaster makes the best copy. The dramatic achievements of the world's first atoms-for-peace conference came as a great surprise to the non-scientific world.

The final conference took place in Geneva in August, 1955. When the delegates sat down for their initial session, several hundred reporters were on hand, although more than two thousand correspondents and photographers had descended on the medieval Swiss city only a month before, to observe the summit meeting between Western and Iron Curtain chiefs of state. That conference may not have produced anything beyond a few shining platitudes, but it was considered far more newsworthy than the deliberations of a few "eggheads" unknown to the rest of the world. This was where the mass circulation press missed a major "beat."

Seventy-three nations sent their foremost scientists to the Geneva atoms-for-peace meeting. Every government represented removed the "secret" label from a staggering amount of priceless nuclear knowledge. Formulae, processes, production methods and machinery hitherto devised only for warfare were now being directed toward constructive ends. Farming, medicine, engineering, transportation, every peaceful human endeavor would benefit. This, said Hammarskjold, was the first step toward a scientific revolution, based on protons and neutrons, that would dwarf the accomplishments of the industrial revolution, based on coal and steam, of the previous century.

The major achievement of the meeting was "a new kind of cooperation among those working in the atomic field," Hammarskjold declared, adding that "this new, highly dynamic element in the world economy" offered a fresh approach to the task of eliminating war by making the ways of peace totally irresistible. The conference, he said, marked the birth of "a new public philosophy concerning the atom." This "public philosophy" was given practical, effective meaning two years later, when the International Atomic Energy Agency was finally created—just as the General Assembly had hoped when it passed the resolution calling for the Geneva Conference.

Of equal importance was the fact that Hammarskjold had brought men of mutually suspicious nations together in a climate of mutual cooperation and good will. Conferences—even scientific conferences—are as old as human relations. But when dozens of countries volunteer to share their scientific secrets in the interest of removing their destructive power, the occasion becomes red-letter event in world history—even if it receives little public attention.

At this time, too, another event strengthened Hammarskjold's belief that there were hopeful signs in the harsh world of international politics. Just before the Geneva conference, he decided to take a few days off to go fishing in the icy waters of his beloved Scandinavian north country. He felt he deserved the brief va-

[100]

cation; after all, it would be a way to celebrate his fif-
tieth birthday.

For some reason the fishing was not good that year,
but the brief interlude of quiet and solitude was extremely welcome. Hammarskjold felt thoroughtly re-
freshed when he returned to his tiny cabin in the village of Skoane. There, he discovered a birthday present
that raised his spirits even higher. Technically it was
not a gift at all, but merely an official cablegram for
the Secretary-General of the United Nations. The sig-
nature on the brief, tersely worded message might have
startled a more excitable man, but Hammarskjold read
it with outward calm, only his blue eyes betraying whatever emotion he felt.

The cable, from the Red Chinese foreign minister,
was a promise that the American airmen would be re-
leased from prison "in the near future."

Perhaps Hammarskjold's usually steady hands
trembled slightly as he folded the message and placed
it carefully in a pocket of his heavy woolen jacket. Here
was news that many of his colleagues had never expected him to receive. Here was incontrovertible evidence that both "quiet diplomacy" and "personal diplomacy" could function with genuine effect for the good
of mankind.

"Many things have happened during my time as
Secretary-General," he later said, "for which I have
reason to be grateful. But no event ranks higher on that
list than my trip to Peiping."

Dag's personal mission to Red China may well have been the turning point in his career as UN chief. He had carried off an incomparable diplomatic coup. Treating with a nation bitterly hostile to the United States, he had nevertheless managed to achieve what the United States wanted. And he had done it without either compromising his strict impartiality or causing the Chinese Communists to lose "face."

After the release of the American airmen, no one ever seriously doubted the potency of Hammarskjold's unique brand of diplomacy. Yet he, himself, often tended to dismiss his ability rather lightly. Once he described his particular talents as "using what brains I have and keeping my mouth shut." Perhaps he paid himself a greater tribute than he realized.

At any rate, the new broom which Dag Hammarskjold had started to wield in the Secretariat building was now demonstrating its effectiveness at the heights of top-level international diplomacy. It would not be long before the Secretary-General was to exchange that broom for a rifle, a rifle to prevent shooting.

Chapter 7

Creating a Force for Peace

Between Port Said on the Mediterranean and Suez on the Red Sea, a distance of about 100 miles over an over-like stretch of desert, runs a large ditch some 65 yards wide. As waterways go, it is not an impressive sight. In terms of world political and economic stability, the Suez Canal may well be the most vital maritime avenue on the globe.

Since its completion in 1869, the Suez Canal had always been a potential powder keg in the seething Middle East. Built by the French, it eventually came under British control. As the key to Britain's lifeline to the Orient, it was the site of a major military and naval base. And despite two world wars, the British always kept the canal open — until 1956.

Egypt's new nationalist government under Colonel

[103]

Gamal Abdel Nasser, was beginning to feel the need to establish itself as a world power. Sensitive over foreign occupation of the Suez area, Egypt put out bids to buy control of the Canal from its British and French stockholders. After protracted talks, it became evident that no agreement could be reached. In October, 1956, Egypt, hypnotized by its own propaganda, broke off negotiations and seized the Canal. Simultaneously, it attacked its archenemy, Israel.

Immediately the tiny Israeli nation struck back, her tough, highly trained troops slicing through the undisciplined Egyptian army like a knife through cheese. Within hours after Israel had launched her counterattack, Britain and France had thrown the might of their ground, sea, and air forces into the full-scale assault against Egypt. It was obviously a matter of perhaps three days at the very most before the three nations would occupy Cairo itself.

Forty-eight hours after it began, the fighting was over. The combined armed might of Britain, France, and Israel had been stopped cold in its tracks, not by the totally demoralized Egyptian army, but by 196 young men armed with nothing but rifles and wearing blue armbands on the sleeves of their uniforms. They had not had to fire a shot.

When the news of the Egyptian invasion first reached Dag Hammarskjold, he came near to displaying open anger. The unexpected British-French-Israeli move had come as that much of a shock to him. For this was more than just another brush-fire border incident. With the Suez Canal as the prize, Hammarskjold knew that the entire world was closer to war than it had been since the end of World War II.

There was a personal element in his distress, too. Perhaps for the only time in his UN career, Hammarskjold felt that he was being betrayed by Britain and France. His emotional and intellectual ties with these nations were closer than with any other country in the United Nations but Sweden. Both countries had led the campaign for his nomination to the Secretary-Generalship in 1953. They had given him vigorous support during the early days when he had sought to strengthen the duties and influence of his office. Now, suddenly, they seemed to have forgotten the simplest meanings of the Charter whose principles they professed to believe in.

After the two nations had stubbornly vetoed two Security Council cease-fire proposals, Hammarskjold left the UN building and drove to his Park Avenue apartment to try to get a few hours of desperately needed rest. But sleep would not come. At dawn the next day, his worried housekeeper found a haggard Secretary-General hunched over his desk, wearily writing out a statement in precise longhand. Several hours later, barely concealling his tension and anger, he went before the Security Council and read his statement. It was courteous and diplomatically worded. It was also an unmistakable offer to resign at once.

"A Secretary-General," said Hammarskjold, managing to keep the tremor out of his voice, "cannot serve on any other assumption than that — within the necessary limits of human frailty and honest differences of opinion — all member-nations honor their pledges and observe all article of the Charter."

The statement was more than an offer to resign; intentionally or not, it was a thinly veiled threat. The principles of the Charter must be respected or the member-nations must be prepared to accept the consequences. And everyone knew the chaos that would result if the Secretary-General were to step down at this crucial hour. The statement produced an immediate, and unanimous, endorsement from every Security Council member. Even the British and French delegates joined their colleagues in refusing to accept the Secretary-General's resignation, despite Hammarskjold's obvious reproaches to their governments — and despite the fact that they had yet to withdraw their troops from Egypt.

Hammarskjold's move had the effect of giving him a freer hand. The British and French could not very well reject UN directions after having just offered such a warm endorsement of the Secretary-General. But fighting had to be stopped in Suez; a major war was still in the making, and Hammarskjold knew he had to act swiftly. Back in his 38th-floor office, he called in the members of the Yugoslav delegation. With them, he drafted a resolution. Approved by the necessary seven Security Council votes, the motion turned the Suez question over to the General Assembly and gave that group authority to take action in the crisis. Having thus received a green light, Hammarskjold then asked Canadian delegate Lester Pearson to join him for lunch.

This was no social get-together. It was scarcely a lunch, for that matter—at least to Hammarskjold. On that day he had little appetite, even for the coffee-flavored ice cream to which he was specially partial. Scarcely noticing his food, he rapidly outlined a motion which he asked Pearson to introduce in the assembly. Briefly, what Hammarskjold wanted was something even more revolutionary and dramatic—and potentially more dangerous—than his delicate personal mission to Red China.

Briefly, he was asking for authority to mobilize a United Nations army.

True, it was not so described. UN troops were to be known as an "emergency force;" their function was to act as police rather than as fighting men, in order to keep the peace in the Suez area and on the Egypt-Israel border. But regardless of its designation, it was to be an army nonetheless. As such, it might shatter forever the prestige of the United Nations if its presence were not respected. Hammarskjold well knew the risk involved in this move. Yet he felt that he had no other choice, even though there was absolutely no precedent for the action under the Charter.

Pearson formally offered the motion to the General Assembly. It was passed, with stipulation that Hammarskjold present a clear plan within 48 hours.

On the basis of the General Assembly action, Israel

[107]

immediately—if reluctantly—agreed to a cease-fire. Hammarskjold then sent urgent messages to Britain and France asking them to follow suit. They too consented, but only at such time as Hammarskjold's promised police force was mobilized for duty.

This time the Secretary-General was not caught off guard by the conditions which Britain and France had laid down. He had already been in touch with the governments of other nations, and he felt confident that his path would not be blocked. All that remained now was to move.

The United Nations map room had once been Ralph Bunche's conference room. With its high ceilings and Spartan furnishings and military air, it must have brought back memories to the Secretary-General. As a child in Sweden, his home had been the ancient Uppsala Castle, where his playroom was a similarly grim, austere chamber. Here, with his brothers, young Dag often played soldier. Somehow, in these games he was invariably cast as a general leading armies against Napoleon. Now it was 1956, and Hammarskjold had in fact become a "general." But his soldiers were no longer toys. The colored pins on the great maps at the UN building represented military forces that dwarfed infire-power any armies that Napoleon could ever have dreamed of mobilizing. If Hammarskjold was playing a game, it was a grim one indeed.

As Bunche, Cordier, and military advisers supplied by delegations pored over maps and prepared troop movements and supply schedules, Hammarskjold picked up a telephone and asked to be put through to the Pentagon in Washington. Half an hour later, U.S. Air Force transport planes were warming up their engines at fields all over Europe. Another eight rapid calls — telephone bills at UN headquarters went into four figures that day — and troops from as many nations were climbing aboard the waiting aircraft. One more call went to the Swiss observer at the UN: "Will it be possible for your government to furnish air transportation for five thousand troops from Capodichine Airport, near Naples, to Suez?"

This was a touchy situation. Hammarskjold did not want American aircraft to fly into Egypt: transportation from the marshaling area in Italy to Suez must be provided by a completely neutral nation. Switzerland, in fact, guarded her neutrality so carefully that she was not even a member of the UN. But the Swiss observer, an old personal friend of Hammarskjold's, said that assistance might be possible in this emergency.

At the airport of Ismailia, an Egyptian town some ten miles from the Suez Canal, a shiny Swissair DC-6B taxied up to the apron. Out of the plane, looking slightly airsick, trooped 45 youthful Danish soldiers wearing sky-blue helmet liners and blue armbands. First Lieutenant Axel Bojsen blinked in the searing Egyptian sunlight, called the men to attention, marched them past the still-smoking ruins of a hangar the British had bombed three days previously, and gave the command to halt and present arms in front of an Egyptian brigadier.

Reviewing UNEF troops at the Abu Suweir airport

"On behalf of the Egyptian armed forces," said
the brigadier in crisp military tones, "I welcome you
as guests, as troops of the United Nations Emergency
Force."

The General Assembly had given Dag Hammarskjold
a free hand in Suez with the time limit almost at zero.
The first contingent of the UN police had landed on
Egyptian soil only 39 hours after the Secretary-General
made his first telephone call. At the end of the day, 196
UNEF troops were on duty in the troubled area. They were

the vanguard of a projected 6,000-man force. Besides the Danes, there were also Norwegians and Colombians. When the latter contingent disembarked at the Abou Suweir air base, their party included a slight-shouldered sandy-haired man in civilian clothes. It was not enough that Dag Hammarskjold should assume all responsibility for bringing this historic force into being. He felt it his duty to be on the spot with the first wave.

The overnight creation of the UNEF was a milestone in the history of Hammarskjold's "impossible" feats. Aside from the delicate and tangled diplomatic obstacles, the peaceful invasion had been an unprecedented masterpiece of last-minute logistics.

Much of the credit for the arrival of the UNEF belonged to Ralph Bunche. It was his responsibility to move the troops of eight different nations from four continents to an undersized, overcrowded marshaling area in southern Italy, and then to fly them another thousand miles to makeshift airstrips scattered all over the Suez area. Tents, vehicles, spare parts, special equipment—literally thousands of tons of supplies—had to be ready not only at Capodochino but also at the Suez bases. Feeding the army - enroute and in Egypt, was a tremendously complicated job. Medical staffs worked in shifts, giving endless immunizations against typhus, smallpox, bilharzia, malaria, cholera, yellow fever. It was also Bunche's job to see that enough serum was on hand, properly labeled, to meet the doctors' needs. Even uniforms proved to be a monumental nuisance.

Helmet liners were hastily provided by the U.S. Army when it was learned at the last minute that the berets which the UN had purchased could not be dyed blue. These were only a few of the innumerable details, large and small, that Bunche had to handle. But somehow he managed to get the job done and carry out his "general's" orders.

It was not long before the United Nations Emergency Force, under the command of Canadian General Redson Burns, had reached its full strength of 6,000, with contingents from Brazil, Canada, Colombia, Denmark, Finland, India, Indonesia, Norway, Sweden and Yugoslavia. Aside from their blue helmet liners, armbands, and shoulder patches, all troops wore the uniforms of their own countries. For the first time in recorded history, an armed alliance had been formed and stood ready, not to conquer or even defend, but to prevent others from fighting.

"Without it," Hammarskjold later said, in one of his habitual understatements, "events would have taken an entirely different and perhaps catastrophic turn."

But there it was, a "force-in-being" which, despite its lilliputian size, was able to avert the full-scale world conflict which the British-French-Israeli invasion had threatened to bring on. For the British and French honored their pledges, and despite a feeling of bitterness at not being allowed to finish what they had started, they removed their troops from Suez. Hammarskjold's principal goal had been achieved.

But a colossal task still faced UNEF, even at full strength. One of its primary responsibilities was to patrol the Egypt-Israeli border. The British and French might have departed, but trouble threatened as long as Nasser and Israeli Premier Ben-Gurion persisted in their refusal to agree to a truce. Compounding the border problem was the Gaza Strip, which had been seized by Israel during the fighting, and which was subsequently returned to Egypt. Meanwhile, the UNEF controlled all movement in this sensitive danger zone.

Refugees were another difficult problem. Camps and hospitals had to be set up for them, and machinery put in motion to rehabilitate them as quickly as possible. U.N. troops also had to supervise the exchange of war prisoners, patrol and clear mine fields, guard power stations, factories, and oil fields from sabotage, and clear and repair damaged roads. They took over certain Egyptian responsibilities, for Egypt had been reduced to a state of near chaos by the invasion. UNEF detachments were called out to prevent riots and looting, and to maintain law and order. For a time they administered some Egyptian prisons, and even operated government switchboards.

One particularly vital job was that of protecting the salvage vessels working in the Suez Canal. The Egyptians had deliberately blocked the waterway by sinking many passenger and cargo ships.

Now it was the responsibility of the United Nations to clear the canal. Anticipating this task, Hammarskjold had been in touch with Dutch and Danish salvage firms. He had also alerted ships and crews from other neutral nations, Belgium, Germany, Italy, Sweden, and Yugoslavia. All were ready when the Secretary-General ordered the clearing operation to begin. It was estimated that this task would take almost a year and cost forty million dollars. By April, 1957, ships were moving through the canal once more. The job had cost less than ten million dollars.

Late in December of 1956, the UNEF was well into its task, functioning swiftly and efficiently. Much of the initial pressure had been taken off the Secretariat. One morning, as Hammarskjold was finishing breakfast, his housekeeper came up to the table and spoke, almost apologetically.

"Please excuse me, Mr. Hammarskjold," she said. "But you have had no rest for weeks. You must at least take a Christmas holdiay."

"Why, of course," smiled the Secretary-General.

He was as good as his word. He spent Christmas in Suez, sharing the Yuletide celebrations with the men who could not go home that year—the troops of the UNEF who had brought peace on earth to men of good will.

For "General" Hammarskjold's army had unquestionable averted war. It is interesting to speculate on what the state of the world might be today if the old League of Nations had had at its disposal a similar force which might have been sent to Ethiopia in 1935.

Perhaps an even greater accomplishment of the UNEF than averting war over Suez was that it finally established the United Nations in the eyes of the world as a *force* for peace. The world body was no longer just another well-intentioned debating society. It had proved that it could and would act.

True, it was not omnipotent; all international differences, unfortunately, would not be resolved as decisively as the Suez crisis. This fact was demonstrated during that same fateful autumn of 1956, when Russian Army tanks rumbled through the streets of Budapest to preserve the Hungarian "people's" government from a handful of ragged, poorly armed reactionaries."

What prevented Hammarskjold from mustering another UNEF for Hungary? One simple fact which can never be overlooked. The United Nations is dedicated to peace. Its "armies" are no stronger than the moral force they command. If a nation disregards this moral force, the UN influence is that much diminished, because it cannot very well start a fight. In the Suez crisis, Britain, France, and Israel withdrew their troops, not before superior numbers, but in the face of a moral force which all three nations respected. In Hungary, however, the Soviets displayed callous indifference to moral considerations of any sort. A UNEF in Budapest might well have served no other purpose than to fan the flames of an already explosive situation.

The UN could accomplish little more in the case of Hungary than a censure of the Soviets. However, few delegates were unaware of the enormous efforts which Hammarskjold exerted to secure justice for the Hungarian freedom fighters, and to negotiate for a solution of the entire Hungarian question. He personally offered to go to Budapest while fighting there was at its heaviest, to see if there was not some way that the Soviets might be induced to withdraw their troops. The offer was coldly spurned. The Red Chinese of two years previously could have given the Kremlin a lesson in courtesy at least. Even this rejection did not discourage Hammarskjold, and during the height of the crisis he worked virtually without sleep for nearly a week. One day he did manage to leave his 38th-floor office at five o'clock in the morning.

Despite the failure of the UN in Hungary, Hammarskjold had produced something new and hopeful from the cauldron of the Suez crisis. This was not just the UNEF, but an intangible that arose from its success. This intangible could be described as a force, an influence, representing the conscience of humanity, which, simply by making itself felt in a trouble spot, will often alleviate that crisis or end it entirely. Hammarskjold had a more direct description of the intangible. He liked to call it "the UN presence."

This "presence" does not necessarily have to consist of 6,000 troops - or even 60. Two years after the Suez emergency, "the UN presence" demonstrated its adaptability to any situation.

On May 22, 1958, Lebanon complained to the Security Council of intervention in its internal affairs by the United Arab Republic. Armed bands from Syria were infiltrating the tiny Lebanese nation. U.A.R. nationals took part in acts of terrorism and rebellion against the established Lebanese government. Weapons were being smuggled in a steady stream across the border from Syria. And all the while, Cairo Radio and the U.A.R. press waged a violent anti-Lebanon propaganda campaign. It was obviously a matter of days before the brush fire could become a holocaust.

Acting on a proposal by Sweden, the UN Security Council immediately dispatched an observer group to the Syria-Lebanon border to insure against any illegal infiltration of arms or personnel between the two countries. The presence of this team enabled the Lebanese government to request United States forces to maintain order, and Marines of the Sixth Fleet hit the beach near Beirut. Without UN representatives on the spot, the presence of U.S. troops would have been unthinkable. Even as things stood, the U.A.R. — and, of course, the Russians, with whom Nasser was becoming more closely allied — screamed "imperialism!" to the skies. But they could do little else, thanks to the handful of United Nations representatives whose job, although technically to observe, was in fact to take all responsibility for stabilizing the precarious situation. The Marines, though under U.S. command, were nevertheless subordinate to the United Nations group. They had landed as a precaution, and had strict orders not to engage in fighting of any kind. Furthermore, it was part of the overall plan that they should withdraw just as soon as the UN representatives could establish stability on the border.

This was a different kind of "presence" indeed. But its very existence prevented hostile governments from exploiting the legitimate arrival of American forces. Eventually, inflamed Arab tempers were calmed. Hammarskjold's mobile, flexible "presence" was thus able to extinguish the sputtering fuse of one more international powder keg.

By now, the "UN presence" had come to be accepted throughout the world as a sort of flying squadron for peace, ready to move at the shortest notice into any trouble spot so long as it could rely on international moral force to back its action.

The "UN presence" had received its basic training in Suez and Lebanon. Now, four thousand miles to the southwest, a series of events was rapidly unfolding to produce a crisis which came close to destroying Dag Hammarskjold — and the entire United Nations. The severest test of the "UN presence" was to take place against the backdrop of an impenetrable rain forest in the heart of Equatorial Africa.

Chapter 8

Congolese Nightmare

Champagne and palm wine flowed in Leopoldville on June 30, 1960, as the bougainvillea-lined avenues of the great city shuddered beneath the frenzied celebrations of several hundred thousand deliriously happy Africans. For this was the day that "independence" had come to the former Belgian Congo, an equatorial region of ten million people, nearly half as large as the United States.

A savage joy permeated the humid tropical atmosphere of the capital city, and relatively minor sour notes were overlooked, such as the incident of a Congolese teen-ager snatching King Baudouin's dress sword as the Belgian ruler drove down the handsome Boulevard Albert I to participate in the transfer-of-government ceremonies. Even the highly offensive behavior of the

the Congo's new premier, goateed Patrice Lumumba, was generally forgotten as a riotous wave of good nature swept the vast country from the Atlantic port of Matadi to the snow-capped Mountains of the Moon, two thousand miles to the east. This was an historic moment. The Republic of the Congo had been born.

Just what the Congolese people would do with their new "independence" was another question. Many citizens expected to preserve it in small bottles sold to them by witch doctors and assorted con men. More sophisticated Congolese thought it meant they would be able to own cars, radios, and enormous mansions. The matter of earning the money to obtain these things was not even a minor detail to them. After all, they had "independence." Did that not automatically assure them of the rights to whatever they wished?

This was roughly the state of affairs in the infant nation on the day that Belgium made the transfer of power. Many experts, even then, warned that the transfer would prove to be the most disastrous abdication of responsibility in the entire history of colonial administrations anywhere. For more than half a century, Belgium had run the Congo as a paternalistic domain in which progress was conspicuous by its total nonexistence. Unlike the British and French, who for decades had been training their colonial peoples toward the day when they would run their own affairs, the Belgians had done nothing to ready the Congolese for "independence." True, there was a facade. One of the colony's proudest showcases was Leopoldville's Lovanium University, which actually boasted an atomic reactor—and a student body of less than two dozen. A young Congolese might consider himself lucky to get as far as high school. Then, almost overnight, the situation changed, as the irresistible tidal wave of African nationalism engulfed the African continent. A few riots in Leopoldville were enough to panic the Belgians into drawing up a constitution which was faultless—on paper. Then they capitulated.

It is no wonder, then, that almost before the ecstatic celebrations had ended, the Republic of the Congo had become an inferno of anarchy and terror. Within two weeks after June 30, the Congolese army mutinied against its Belgian officers, and went on a spree of pillage, rape, and murder almost unequaled in Africa's bloody annals. Terror-stricken Belgian families streamed into Leopoldville from every part of the country. They crowded aboard ferries, and made their way to safety in the city of Brazzaville, just across the Congo River.

At the same time, the province of Katanga seceded from the Republic, proclaiming its own independence, and setting off the chain of events whcih, a little over a year later, was to culminate in the death of Dag Hammarskjold. The secessionist move, sparked by Moise Tshombe, also deprived the remainder of the new nation of immeasurable mineral wealth in copper and cobalt. (Katanga had provided more than two-thirds of Congo revenue in the past.) Tribal rivalries in vast bush regions, suppressed for years by the Belgians, suddenly burst forth in horrifying warfare and mass murder. Yet "independence" was still sweet—on paper.

This was the situation Dag Hammarskjold found himself faced with as he walked into the map room of the Secretariat one morning early in July, 1960. He had just received a cable from Prime Minister Lumumba and Congo President Joseph Kasavubu, urgently requesting UN military assistance to restore order in the collapsing nation. The Secretary-General was not entirely unprepared for this turn of events. His personal representative, Ralph Bunche, had been working hard in Leopoldville since June 30, arranging for badly needed technical assistance. There were scarcely any Congolese administraters, lawyers, engineers, or agricultural experts. There were no doctors at all. The only specialty in abundance seemed to be political demagoguery.

The UN program of technical and financial aid had been looked on as a rare ray of hope in the Congo. But now there was an even more desperate need, for technicians would be of little value in a country rapidly reverting to primitive savagery. Even Lumumba seemed to recognize the importance of the "UN presence."

With his military advisers, Hammarskjold carefully studied large-scale maps of the Congo. Isolating the principal trouble spots and relating them to the proximity of other African nations, he returned to his own office and set to work on a mobilization schedule. Then he picked up the telephone.

"Please connect me with Flagstaff House in Accra,"
he said to the UN operator. "I wish to speak with Prime
Minister Nkrumah, personally."

This was the start of a long-distance telephone

UN flag flutters over troops protecting the Gaza Strip

marathon that surpassed by several hours the calls put
in by Hammarskjold during the Suez emergency four
years earlier. When the Secretary-General finally put
down the receiver, he had spoken to the chiefs of state of

[*123*]

a half dozen African nations, as well as those of Sweden and Canada. All had told him that troops would be placed at the disposal of the United Nations immediately, provided transportation were furnished. Hammarskjold smiled. An aide had already spoken to the Pentagon and arranged for U.S. Air Force cooperation. Private airlines had also been arranged for.

Within 24 hours, troops from Ghana, wearing the now familiar blue helmet liners and armbands, were pouring from the bellies of huge air transports at Ndjili Airport in Leopoldville. Sabena and SAS jets were circling the field with Swedish detachments. A thousand miles to the east, a gaudily-marked Ethiopian Airlines DC-6B was dropping down over the dense Congo rain forest, to land at the Stanleyville airport and discharge the first contingents of Ethiopia's Imperial Guard — tough, battle-hardened Korean war veterans. In short order, over 10,000 African and European soldiers in full battle dress were patrolling the streets of "Leo" and "Stan," fighting through bush and jungle on scouting parties in northern Katanga, and standing guard on the great Mississippi-type steamers that plied the Congo River.

Once more, Dag Hammarskjold's "UN presence" was making itself felt.

It would be good to record that the arrival of the UN police force brought order to the stricken Congo that summer. This, unfortunately, is not what happened. It has already been pointed out that the strength of the "UN presence" depends largely on the recognition of moral force by the country or countries involved in the UN operation. But moral force, as it is generally understood in the free world, was relatively unknown to the uneducated and undisciplined Congolese army, whose troops switched allegiances with clockwork regularity as they continued their drunken orgy of intimidation and violence. And as far as the warring tribes of the interior were concerned, the only moral force they could understand was stone-age brutality.

Moreover, these difficulties were compounded by some of the very Congolese leaders who had pleaded so desperately for UN assistance. To Lumumba in particular, it rapidly became apparent that his plans for power were being threatened by a force whose only concern was to restore order, regardless of whose political ambitions might be thwarted in the process. Operating on the totalitarian principle that "those who are not for me are against me," Lumumba found the UN's strict neutrality intolerable. So in short order, he discarded even the facade of statesmenship for undisguised rabble-rousing. He shouted the well-worn nationalist threat that if the Western powers did not provide proper recognition and assistance, he would "seek elsewhere."

In particular, he launched an all-out barrage against Dag Hammarskjold, accusing the Secretary-General of misinterpreting Security Council directives and of taking orders from the Belgians. His indictments reached a ludicrous peak when he declared that Hammarskjold had a secret understanding with the Belgian government, based on what he claimed to be a relationship by marriage between the Swedish and Belgian royal families.

At this fantastic allegation, Dag could only shrug and suppress a smile.

But Lumumba persisted. When Hammarskjold visited Katanga with a UN team, the fire-eating Congo premier demanded that he postpone his return to New York until he, Lumumba, could accompany the UN party with a Congolese delegation to the world group.

"He even insisted that Dag make room for him on the plane," recalled a newspaperman who was in Leopoldville at the time.

Hammarskjold's reply was a courteous but firm memorandum to Lumumba, pointing out that this procedure was altogether out of order.

Not fazed, Lumumba stepped up the pace of his inflammatory behavior. Like many a demagogue before him he exploited race hatred to the fullest. On the pretext that they were seeking out "Belgian spies," troops loyal to Lumumba attacked Europeans of every nationality. Canada issued a furious protest when several Royal Canadian Air Force technicians were brutally beaten at Ndjili Airport. A U.S. Air Force crew was stomped into insensibility at Stanleyville, seat of Lumumba's rise to power.

Such unbridled savagery created a touchy situation in the UN command itself. General Alexander, the British officer commanding the Ghanaian contingent, complained bitterly that soldiers could not be considered soldiers if they were not allowed to fight back. A high ranking UN officer in Stanleyville declared that he would personally shoot any Congolese soldier whom he caught molesting a foreign civilian. Dag Hammarskjold's principle of rigid impartiality was being sorely tried. Yet despite the frustration felt by trained fighting men, the UN force maintained its neutrality. As the Secretary-General well knew, it often takes far more courage to turn the other cheek than to fight back.

Finally, responsible Congolese leaders became seriously disturbed by Lumumba's intemperate ravings. Late in August, the bespectacled, deceptively mild-mannered Colonel Joseph D. Mobutu staged a lightning military coup in Leopoldville. Seizing power, he proclaimed that the Congolese government would henceforth be run by President Kasavubu and a "College of Commissioners." Kasavubu immediately ordered the Soviet and Czech embassies to close. He gave their staffs 24 hours to get out of the country. Lumumba, although technically still Premier, was powerless.

This was the background against which the General Assembly opened its 15th session in September, 1960. From the start, it promised to be a stormy gathering, for the Soviet Union had discovered in the Congo tragedy — and in Patrice Lumumba — the opportunity it had been seeking for decades; a foot in the door on the African continent. Thus no one was unduly surprised at the announcement that Nikita Khrushchev himself would come to New York with the Soviet delegation. It was

[127]

even less surprising that he was followed by all his satellite leaders. The Iron Curtain was marshaling its might to make its strongest bid in the history of the United Nations.

Dag Hammarskjold opened the door of his 38th-floor office — which faces the East River — crossed the conference room and glanced at the Picasso painting on the wall. Then he stepped into the adjoining reception room and looked down from the window. Below, on First Avenue, the cordons of police flanking the UN building resembled regiments of blue ants. Thousands of equally tiny spectators packed the other side of the street as the continuing wail of sirens announced the arrival of delegation after delegation, each with its own police motorcycle escort. Suddenly, a loud, angry murmur carried up to the 38th floor. A demonstration, chiefly of captive nation citizens, was in full blast. It was time for the Secretary-General to proceed to the General Assembly Hall.

Premier Khrushchev had reason to be confident as he took his seat among the Soviet delegates in the great General Assembly hall. After all, the Soviet Union was about to extend its vast empire into Africa. The Congo was prostrate, torn by ignorance, poverty, tribal rivalries, and feuding political ambitions. (Two separate Congolese delegations had arrived in New York, each seeking UN recognition. Neither got it.) Total national collapse was the classic opening wedge for any major Communist move.

In Lumumba, the Communists had the perfect quisling. Further, Khrushchev thought he could rely on overwhelming support in the General Assembly itself. That year, eighteen newly independent African nations had been admitted to UN membership. All were former colonies and had no love for "imperialism." Khrushchev was also counting on Ghana and Guinea. Kwame Nkrumah's "neutralism" was steadily being diluted with scathing attacks on the West, and Guinea's Sekou Toure seldom concealed his almost worshipful admiration of Marxism. The Afro-Asian block could scarcely fail to give all-out support to Russia's position, Khrushchev felt. The satellite nations, of course, were already in the bag. A majority was inevitable. All that remained now was to launch an all-out assault on "imperialism"—in the person of Dag Hammarskjold.

For it was the "UN presence" alone, Hammarskjold's own creation, that stood in the way of a Soviet takeover in the Congo. Despite many failures and setbacks in the job of trying to keep order, the UN troops and UN technical assistance programs had made themselves felt as a moral force throughout the free world. But Khrushchev was not concerned with the free world. He was out to grab the Congo, and he would do it with a scapegoat, Dag Hammarskjold.

Khrushchev sat in his seat at the General Assembly, and listened cheerfully as the Soviet's Valerian A. Zorin excoriated Hammarskjold and his "imperialist" Congo policy.

"The UN command, and the Secretary-General in particular," shouted Zorin, "ignore the lawful government of the Congo." Hammarskjold, he declared, was functioning purely "as a supine tool of the colonial powers." Zorin went on in this vein for more than an hour, concluding with the demand that the delegates censure Hammarskjold and sharply restrict his authority as Secretary-General.

Zorin's tirade was not without effect, but many "sure" delegates did not yet seem sufficiently aroused. Accordingly, Khrushchev himself mounted the podium.

Even his bitterest foe had to concede that the man knew how to deliver a stem-winder in the grand manner, as Khrushchev hurled blast after blast at Hammarskjold. He accused the Secretary-General of "trying to justify the bloody crimes against the Congolese people by the colonialists and their stooge." The "gallant leader," Lumumba, he roared, was being stripped of authority in Hammarskjold's insidious scheme to restore Belgian oppression and to bring back a reign of imperialist tyranny. The performance was a lengthy materpiece of verbal fury, and through it all Dag, the "villain" of the piece, sat quietly, his head slightly bent, his face betraying no emotion. Occasionally he toyed with a pencil or consulted a file. Finally, Khrushchev finished, took his seat, and waited to pick up the pieces.

But nothing was broken. The Soviets had seriously miscalculated the free African nations, who perversely took the word "independence" in its literal meaning, and gave Hammarskjold and the "UN presence" an overwhelming endorsement. Even some of the countries which Khrushchev thought he had in his pocket showed that they, too, had minds of their own. Nkrumah strongly reaffirmed Ghana's dedication to the principles of the UN Charter, and a wave of pleased astonishment swept through the hall when Sékou Touré got up and publicly chastised Khrushchev for what he described as a shocking display of bad manners.

The Russian strategy had backfired badly. Round one went to Dag Hammarskjold – by a near knockout.

But the fight was far from over. The Soviets continued to lay down their barrage of invective as the tempo of events in the Congo became swifter. Early in November, Lumumba suddenly vanished from Leopoldville. Rumors flashed through the rain forest faster than the beat of the African "talking drums." He had gone to Stanleyville to organize an opposition government. He was conferring with Nasser in Cairo. He was Khruschev's personal guest in the Kremlin. Several days later he returned to Leopoldville – a prisoner of Colonel Mobutu's troops.

Highly reliable sources reported that Lumumba was being savagely beaten every day. Hammarskjold, who had taken more personal abuse from this man than from anyone save Khrushchev himself, launched an angry protest to the Kasavubu-Mobutu government. He took steps to contact Lumumba personally through the International Red Cross.

Meanwhile, Lumumba sympathizers in Stanleyville retaliated by holding all Europeans there as hostages. Russia intensified her demand that "the legitimate people's government of the Congo" be recognized. Smallpox epidemics broke out in Kasai and Katanga, adding to the agony of the tribal warfare that raged unchecked in those regions. When the 15th General Assembly finally ended its regular session in December, the Congo's "freedom" was a tragic mockery.

The weeks wore on. President John F. Kennedy was inaugurated and Adlai Stevenson became the new U.S. Ambassador to the UN. One of Lumumba's Stanleyville puppets threatened to behead all hostages. Three "neutral" nations—Morocco, the U.A.R., and Indonesia—announced the withdrawal of their troops from the UN Congo force. Sweden followed suit, for different reasons. Members of an Irish contingent in northern Katanga were ambushed, killed, and their bodies savagely mutilated. The Congolese army itself was split down the middle, with a large Lumumba force gathering in Stanleyville. The country, deprived of Katanga's wealth, hovered on the brink of bankruptcy, and the specter of famine stalked the land.

Late in the evening of February 12, 1961, Dag Hammarskjold was poring over several voluminous reports at his desk. He had had a trying day, but it was imperative that he prepare memoranda to be ready for his aides the following morning. Sleep would have to wait. There was a knock on his door. A white-lipped

[*132*]

secretary entered with a cable.

Patrice Lumumba, attempting to escape from prison, had been killed near the Katanga border.

Here was Russia's second big chance. Lumumba immediately became a martyr. Lumumba's Stanleyville government was officially recognized by the Soviets and their satellites. "Spontaneous" anti-UN demonstrations took place in a dozen cities on four continents. At the New York headquarters, a flurry of violence interrupted Adlai Stevenson's first major speech before the world group.

The principal target of Russia's new campaign, of course, was Dag Hammarskjold. He had been given many nicknames in his career as Secretary-General; some affectionate, others less so. But it took the Soviets to come up with the word "murderer." It was only to be expected that they would hold him personally responsible for Lumumba's death. They had no intention of failing in their Congo ambitions a second time.

Round Two opened at the now-famous General Assembly session at which the Soviet delegation demanded Hammarskjold's resignation and replacement by a three-man "troika" commission. The round ended almost as quickly as it had begun, as the Secretary-General won his thumping 70-0 vote of confidence.

This vote brought on a showdown. The Soviets, in a cold, savage fury, made their next move. They had not been able to browbeat Hammarskjold, so they immediately switched to a new strategy. Shortly after their

[133]

Visiting Congo officials, trying to end civil war

defeat in the General Assembly, the Russians received an invitation to a luncheon being given by Hammarskjold for Ghana's Nkrumah. Zorin did not even trouble to reply. In effect, he said: "How can we acknowledge an invitation from a person who does not exist?" In short, the Russians were determined to ostracize Hammarskjold. They were out to get him, just as they had got Trygve Lie.

As far as the Congo was concerned, however, the back of the Communist strategy seemed to have been broken, for aside from continuing support of the Stanleyville government, now under Antoine Gizenga, their assaults on the "UN presence" seemed to diminish. They did not even make a serious attempt to block the resolution of February 21, which authorized UN troops to use force "as a last resort" to restore order in the demoralized Kasavubu government.

Despite the new free hand given to the Secretary-General, the UN task was still terrifyingly far from complete. Bankruptcy loomed larger every day. Hammarskjold's urgent request for an emergency grant of one hundred and thirty-five million dollars to meet the Congo's barest needs was cooly received. The Soviets had never contributed, and now France balked. Only the U.S., Britain, and Canada managed to save the day with their contributions. The pressure of opposition was increasing in Katanga, where president Moise Tshombe consistently spurned Hammarskjold's demands that he oust his Belgian advisers and army officers. The dangerous shortage of UN troops continued, but when India offered its own forces, the Kasavubu government balked violently. Real fighting broke out when Sudanese UN troops were driven from the port of Matadi by Congolese forces. It seemed as if the Congo nightmare would never end.

But a small break in the clouds came in April of 1961, when representatives of opposing Congolese factions met at Tananarive, capital of the Malagasy Republic on the island of Madagascar. Sparked by Katanga's Tshome, they reached agreement on a loose confederation of states which might reunite the dissension-torn land. This was not a perfect arrangement and the leftist Gizenga rejected it, but at least it was a start. Even with the subsequent arrest of Tshombe, it was generally felt that perhaps negotiation would gradually remove the threat of civil war. Tshombe's continued difiance after his release and return to Katanga did not dispel the growing optimism in the Congo. And when more negotiation · finally produced a meeting of the Congolese parliament in late July, Dag Hammarskjold must have enjoyed his black cigar a bit more than usual. Certainly he and his colleagues had a right to look back on a substantial amount of achievement after the previous 12 months' ordeal.

Much had been done by the "UN presence." Here are only a few of its accomplishments:

"An international staff of 750 officers undertook to prevent the collapse of essential services. UN experts took over the major hospitals, distributed food, kept the largest airports open and manned the communications system. By the end of June, 1,000 Congolese were enrolled in training programs within the Congo and 90 had been sent abroad for study. A Monetary Council was set up as the country's basic financial authority. A six-month training course on farm mechanics was set up. An education crash program has provided 64 teachers for vital posts. A public works program is under way to carry out basic maintenance and to relieve unemployment. About 100 medical specialists from 20 countries are at work in the Congo."

The UN itself has described these accomplishments as merely a start. Yet considering the difficulties facing Hammarskjold in organizing the monumental Congo rescue operation—transporting thousands of tons of food, clothing, and medical supplies, recruiting skilled personnel from nearly 100 nations, keeping the supply and communication lines open in the face of frequent opposition from the very government for which the UN was working—the "start" of technical assistance in the Congo was only slightly short of a colossal achievement.

There was more good news, too, on the political front. After displaying a suitable amount of outrage at the new session of the Congolese parliament, Moise Tshombe presently changed his tune, and Katanga was on its way back to the fold of an increasingly unified Congo. But the most astonishing about-face of all came early in August, when Antoine Gizenga called the envoys of the Iron Curtain nations into his office and informed them that the Stanleyville government no longer existed. He would henceforth serve as vice-premier in the Leopoldville regime under president Kasavubu and newly elected premier, Cyrille Adoula.

Although staggering tasks obviously remained before the Congo would function as a genuinely independent nation, even the most hardened skeptic could now hope that Dag Hammarskjold had pulled the patient through its year of agonized crisis. Yet gratifying as these developments must have been to the Secretary-General himself, he would have found little opportunity, even if he sought it, for self-congratulation. The African continent was still at the boil. A UN commission was desperately seeking entry into Portuguese Angola against a background of anti-colonial violence that made Kenya's Mau Mau rebellion look mild by comparison. Another team was making even less headway in its efforts to investigate conditions in South West Africa. The medieval practice of apartheid racial segregation in South West Africa threatened to bring on another hurricane of tribal revolt, yet both South Africa and Portugal persistently rebuffed Hammarskjold's conciliatory moves by accusing the UN of interference in "domestic" affairs.

Then, too, while the Congo emergency was cooling off, another crisis broke out on Africa's northernmost tip. In one of the most serious brush fire conflicts since the Korean war, French paratroops, protected by bombers and an offshore artillery barrage, invaded Tunisia. The bone of contention was the French naval base at Bizerte. Tunisian President Bourguiba's somewhat high-handed demand for immediate French evacuation of the base brought on the equally senseless full-scale armed assault that threatened to force pro-Western Bourguiba into the arms of Nasser and the increasingly powerful Arab League.

Characteristically, Hammarskjold instantly assumed responsibility, and stepped into the breach. He flew directly to Tunisia with an eye to applying his celebrated personal diplomacy before the dispute got out of hand altogether. The same France that had so enthu-

[138]

siastically nominated him eight years before now handed him the rudest possible rebuff. When his car, flying the blue UN flag, was halted by a French sentry outside Bizerte, Hammarskjold immediately identified himself. The Legionnaire was unmoved.

"I'm sorry, monsieur," he said, with almost sarcastically elaborate courtesy, "but my orders are to allow no unauthorized civilians beyond this post."

Another man might have taken this as a personal affront. Dag Hammarskjold was interested only in ending hostilities in one more trouble spot. Immediately he cabled Paris, and requested a conference there. The French, adding to the previous insult, refused pointblank. Once more, hostility toward Hammarskjold seemed to depend on whose ox was being gored.

Yet for all the "impossible" obstacles produced by Africa's ceaseless unrest and violence, one development of incalculable significance – and hope – for the future of the world had emerged. This was the immeasurable increased stature of the "UN presence."

Hammarskjold had been subjected to severe criticism when he ordered UN troops not to fight in the Congo. He had also been ridiculed when the Sudanese forces were beaten in Matadi. Large units of the UNEF had packed up and quit because their countries found keeping the peace to be inconsistent with their own political ambitions. Two of the Secretary-General's personal representatives were virtually forced from the Congo by the government the UN was trying to preserve from dissolution. But somehow, the UNEF survived. Indeed, it did more than that. For when the shouts and threats died down, when the smoke cleared, the world saw the beginning of a new Congo arising from the ruins. The infant nation had come through its ordeal of fire, thanks to 20,000 men wearing blue helmet liners and blue armbands.

It may be a long time before Dag Hammarskjold's UNEF is automatically obeyed as the police force of the world. But today more than ever, nations are learning what power lies behind the words "moral force" when it has an instrument like the "UN presence" to give it practical and purposeful application.

Chapter 9

A Day in the Secretariat

Every day in New York several million alarm clocks jangled and several million New Yorkers yawned and rubbed their eyes in preparation for another day. But by the time most of these people had awakened, Dag Hammarskjold was well into his work at his office in the UN building.

The Secretary-General's day began early and ended late. By the time he had finished breakfast, he had also read four newspapers from cover to cover, putting pencil marks around items which had bearing on the decisions he would have to make during the day. At especially busy or very critical times, he spent the night in a small bedroom adjoining his office.

Everyone remembers the exciting role the Secretary-General played in such dramas as the liberation of the

American flyers from Red China, the 11th-hour recruiting of a "peace army" to prevent full-scale war at the Suez Canal, and the desperate intervention to stave off chaos in the rain forest of the Congo. But the business of quenching global holocausts was only one part of Hammarskjold's job. The less glamorous side of the Secretary-General's responsibility was as unfamiliar to the General public as the other side of the moon.

Every morning Hammarskjold faced a mountain of papers on his desk. He might well have compared himself with the president of a giant corporation. Hammarskjold's "firm" was preoccupied with two and a half billion "customers" — the entire population of the world.

It would probably be more accurate to compare the Secretary-General's job with that of the President of the United States. For Hammarskjold, in many respects, was chief executive of the globe. And his vast organization is not unlike our own governmental apparatus. Its Charter was modeled on the U.S. Constitution. Its administrative and governing machinery roughly follows the pattern of the American checks-and-balances system. Executive responsibility lies largely with the Secretary-General. The Security Council and General Assembly can be likened in some ways to our Senate and House of Representatives, although their legislative function takes the form of recommendations. The General Assembly, like our House of Representatives, holds the purse strings. Judicial matters of the UN are in the hands of the International Court of Justice - somewhat hampered, it is true, by what Hammarskjold described as "self-defeating reservations against its jurisdiction," but nonetheless a truly international judiciary.

In a large sense, the United Nations is a nation unto itself. Although situated in midtown Manhattan, it is technically international territory. Americans visiting the building are on "foreign" soil. The UN has its own internal government, which included police and fire departments and a bank. Like any sovereign nation, it has its own postal administration, which issues stamps that can be posted only in the UN building. A special commemorative stamp in honor of Dag Hammarskjold was in manufacture at the UN printery even before his interrment.

The more than two thousand typewriters in the Secretariat are equipped with keyboards in two dozen different languages. Of course the United Nations itself has five official languages—English, French, Spanish, Russian and Chinese—but its office of Public Information works in a multiplicity of tongues. For Chinese, there is a special team of caligraphers copying the translations. Switchboard operators, specially picked for their command of foreign tongues, can place calls in Hindi, Chinese, or Turkish. And, of course, a batalion of interpreters in soundproof glass booths is always on hand during Council and Assembly sessions, translating speeches from a variety of languages almost as rapidly as they are delivered.

This highly cosmopolitan machinery can be baffling

Being greeted at New Delhi by Prime Minister Nehru of India

to the uninitiated. Dr. Ralph Bunche, formerly Hammarskjold's special aide and later head of UN operations in the Congo, told about a lady visitor from the Midwest who sat down to rest after making an extensive tour of the UN building. Dr. Bunche went over to her and asked if there was anything he might do for her.

"No thanks," the lady replied, "I've had a marvelous day. There's only one question I'd like to ask, though. How is it that the UN is being run by so many furriners?"

The "furriners" in the Secretariat include many

Americans, but all employes - unlike delegates to the Security Council and General Assembly - must take a special oath of allegiance to the UN, regardless of their nationality. This oath is required under the Charter. Thus, a French health expert, an American economist, a Japanese agricultural specialist, all acquire new "citizenship" as members of the Secretariat. The regulation never calls for any act that would compromise an individual's loyalty to his own country, but while on the Secretariat staff, no employe can receive instructions from his own government. Hammarskjold, an intensely patriotic Swede, was almost painfully conscientious in applying this rule to himself.

As "president of the world," Hammarskjold guided the machinery of a sprawling global operation. He dealt with a multiplicity of agencies with headquarters in a dozen world capitals, and branches and subdivisions in the most far-flung and isolated spots of the earth. UN missions can be found in almost 90 countries, to say nothing of the 28 UN information centers in as many capitals. This vast apparatus is charged with bettering mankind's condition in every single walk of life, and as such, they comprised the bulk of Hammarskjold's work. True, their operations seldom make headlines; more often than not, they do not even rate newspaper coverage. Yet it would be impossible to overestimate their significance as a force for universal well-being. There is undeniable excitement in flying to some trouble spot and personally preventing the outbreak of a war, but the less glamorous task of making peace worthwhile is every bit as vital to the interests of humanity. This is the conscience of the world in action, and the final responsibility for guiding it and making it work rested with Dag Hammarskjold.

During any typical week at the UN, Hammarskjold was directly involved in a multitude of small problems. Here are only a few of the questions he had to answer.

How can a program of schoolroom inoculation against cholera be expedited in Saudi Arabia? This was a project of UNICEF, the United Nations Children's Fund. (When the fund was first established in 1946, the "E" stood for "emergency"; the initial remains). Its aid directly reaches some 55 million children and mothers in more than 100 countries, especially in less advanced parts of the world, where a youngster's chances of reaching adolescence are slim. UNICEF had vaccinated 14 million children against tuberculosis, treated three million for yaws, two million for trachoma and other eye diseases, and nearly a million for leprosy. It furnishes basic medical supplies for maternal and child health centers. These basic supplies include powdered milk and vitamins used in supplementary feedings as well as equipment to dry local dairy products such as buffalo milk in India and goat's milk in Greece.

Through hospitals, health centers, and long-range nutrition programs established by UNICEF, child mortality and illness all over the globe is steadily being reduced. Where does UNICEF get its funds? From voluntary contributions exclusively, solicited in innumerable ways.

Should funds be allocated for a long-range study of the Swollen Shoot blight which affects cocoa trees? That question would come from the Food and Agricultural Organization (F.A.O.), charged with seeing to it that the world's increasing populations gets enough to eat. Through F.A.O. efforts, millions of square miles of exhausted and inexpertly-worked land are being revitalized with modern scientific farming. Training programs are set up for Mexican peasants, Indonesian rice farmers, Uganda coffee growers, and Ivory Coast fishermen. These programs are raising the output levels of smaller nations from bare subsistence to a decent standard of living. Crop rotation, chemical fertilizers, machinery for plowing, seeding spraying and reaping, new breeding and hatchery methods, all these are helping to produce a greater yield of the earth's agricultural wealth.

Should there be a literacy requirement for voters in Ruanda-Urundi? Here Hammarskjold would have dealt with the UN Trusteeship Council, which guides the progress of the Trusteeship Territories - Ruanda-Urundi, Tanganyika, and a number of South Pacific islands. Once German colonies, these countries became League of Nations Mandated Territories after World War I, and were put under UN jurisdiction in 1945. The territories are administered principally by Britain, Belgium, and the U. S., who must make periodic reports on their stewardship to the United Nations, with an eye to granting independence on established target dates. Okinawa, in this category, is an American problem, and the question of its independence will be coming up for solution very soon. Ruanda-Urundi may be the Trusteeship Council's biggest headache. This central African land is appallingly overpopulated (five million inhabitants in an area of 20,000 square miles), it has no economy to speak of, and its Belgian administrators fear that independence may bring on a small-scale repetition of the Congo disaster. Thus a question on the franchise might well mean the difference between order and chaos in this tiny, strife-torn country.

What is the potential agricultural yield from a proposed dam and hydroelectric plant on the Niger River? A conference with officials of the United Nations Special Fund would have given Hammarskjold the answer. They assist underdeveloped nations in launching agricultural and industrial programs largely through research. Before any country can move ahead with a specific project, it must know which of its resources can be developed most profitably, and the Special Fund conducts the appropriate studies.

The Special Fund is one of several such funds responsible for helping new or "have-not" nations on the road to economic stability. All these organizations are subsidiary in one way or another to the International Bank for Reconstruction and Development, which has lent over $5 billion since its founding in 1945. New hydroelectric power plants in Mexico, modern highways in Ethiopia, steel mills in India, a nuclear power plant is southern Italy, a huge new harbor in the port of Rangoon, Burma – these are a few economic improvements made possible by International Bank loans. The Bank's funds come almost entirely from members' subscriptions to capital shares; in 1960, total subscribed capital was nearly $20 billion. Here Dag Hammarskjold's could bring his vast experience in banking and economics to the problems at hand.

Can several hundred Iron Curtain refugees be resettled in Australia? This might be a proposal of the United Nations Relief and Works Agency (U.N.R.W.A.), dedicated to helping people who have been victims of political persecution or natural disaster. U.N.R.W.A. plays friend-in-need to 850,000 homeless, chronically ill, aged and handicapped men, women and children. It maintains camps and sponsors housing construction, operates health and sanitation programs. It does not function as a charity. By sponsoring agricultural developments, it enables refugee communities to maintain economic independence - and keep their self-respect. It encourages children toward a decent future primary and elementary education is offered to 180,000 boys and girls, with scholarships for the more promising teen-agers. Probably its most important task is relocating displaced families and giving them an entirely new start with a clean and hopeful slate. Hence the proposal that Australian farm country might be able to accommodate

[*149*]

some of these people and help restore meaning to their lives.

How can a program of recruiting student nurses in South Vietnam be stepped up? Subjects such as this are the province of the World Health Organization (W.H.O.), history's first full-time international medical service. W.H.O.'s job is that of any hospital – except on a global scale. Prevention and cure, research, establishment of international standards for drugs and vaccines, organization and staffing of clinics, training personnel, furnishing information – these W.H.O. services are provided to 144 different governments and territories. They know that progress will slack off without more trained doctors, nurses, public health experts and technicians. Carefully worked out recruiting programs are a vital part of W.H.O.'s $17 million budget, supplied by 90 member-nations.

Should portable film units be used for adult education in Pakistan? The agency Hammarskjold would have consulted on this problem is the United Nations Education, Scientific and Cultural Organization (U.N.E.S.C.O.), which works toward a three-pronged goal: Providing full and equal educational opportunities, harnessing science in the service of mankind as a whole and making the rewards of culture available to everyone. Ignorance, more than anything else, breeds war, and today, more than 45 percent of the world's adults can neither read nor write. Scientific progress over the past half century has been staggering, yet mankind benefits from only

[150]

a microscopic fraction of these advances. The exchange of culture – literature, painting, music – plays a great part in cementing international good will and understanding. Hence U.N.E.S.C.O.'s worldwide program of free, compulsory education, its sponsorship of meetings like the International Atomic Energy Conference, which was described in an early chapter, and its many student and teacher exchange programs. A $13 million annual budget falls fantastically short of meeting U.N.E.S.C.O.'s needs, but the very existence of this inique agency is a major step forward. It shows the recognition that man does not live by bread alone.

These are only seven out of literally hundreds of questions which Hammarskjold handled every week. And the agencies mentioned are only part of the Secretariat structure.

Hammarskjold's work with these agencies was plodding. It called for an intimate knowledge of countless small details. It required the Secretary-General's presence at endless conferences. It demanded that he read report after voluminous report. Such responsibilities obviously have little – if any – of the drama and suspence of high-level international politics. Yet they make up what may well prove in the long run to be the most important part of the United Nations operation. For in agencies dedicated to the health and the well-being of individuals, the U. N. is declaring that world peace does not only mean freedom from war; it also embodies the words of our own Declaration of Inde-

pendence: 'life, liberty and the pursuit of happiness."
This is the goal toward which Dag Hammarskjold worked
in the lesser known side of his job as Secretary-General. And it's very likely that history will honor his efforts
to coordinate the UN job with the work of these agencies
long after the bitter fights in the Security Council and
General Assembly have been forgotten.

Chapter 10

The Many-sided Hammarskjold

At about eight o'clock every evening, when Dag Hammarskjold finished his work at the Secretariat and stepped into the street, be became another person. He was no longer the legally precise, impersonal Secretary-General that millions saw on television. He was Dag Hammarskjold, human being.

Nearly everyone knows that Hammarskjold was an inordinately shy man. This fact, and the normal demands of diplomacy, generally caused him to put on an expressionless, poker-faced front that was impossible to penetrate. Associates tried vainly to catch his mood by watching such signs as a raised eyebrow or a nearly imperceptible twist at the corner of his mouth.

Although a "clean desk man" − souvenir hunters could never make off with anything but a paper knife -

he nevertheless worked in his shirtsleeves behind a thick cloud of tobacco smoke from the pipe or black cigarillos which he smoked incessantly. He had no affectations. His clothes were ready-made, and the only noticeable part of his attire was the almost inevitable bow tie. He never wore a hat, no matter what the weather.

No one, it is true, could reach Hammarskjold's inner feelings uninvited, but at the same time no one ever felt unwelcome in his presence. One day, during the heat of the Lebanon crisis, he took a taxi from the UN to his East Side apartment. The driver, recognizing his celebrated passenger, immediately launched into a long catalog of complaints about traffic conditions around the Secretariat building. Hammarskjold - at that moment searching his mind for some measure which might keep the Middle East from exploding - listened politely to the driver, and offered one or two suggestions. At the end of the trip, the driver said: "Listen, Mr. Hammerhold, forget my griping, huh? It was a pleasure taking you home."

A dedicated diplomat with a driving singleness of purpose on the job, Hammarskjold actually had two different private lives; indoor and outdoor. When he arrived home, he took up the refined pursuits of the intellectual. Regardless of what crisis may have been hovering over the UN Hammarskjold made an almost religious point of reading at least three hours every evening, his library was easily the most lived-in of any room in his apartment. He once said that the Bible,

[154]

Shakespeare and – oddly enough – "Don Quixote" – are the three indispensable books for any person who would pretend to culture. But he himself also roamed as far afield as Jack Kerouac. As a member of the Nobel Prize Committee, he conscientiously read every single literary work submitted for consideration.

High on the list of his personal literary preferences were T. S. Eliot, James Joyce, Thomas Wolfe, Joseph Conrad, Marcel Proust, Thomas Mann and St.-John Perse – the latter occupying a special niche in Hammarskjold's estimation because Perse gave up a diplomatic career for poetry.

In 1960, the Secretary-General translated Perse's "Chronicles" from the French. "Isn't it an amazing thought," a friend commented, "that the man who had the Congo on his hands in August, and Khrushchev on his back in October, could still find rest and pleasure in polishing the manuscript before sending it home to Sweden for publication? Surely this is one of his many secret weapons." Hammarskjold himself described poetry as "intellectual calisthenics". Friends said it was no myth that he once stood on a mountaintop reciting Eliot's "The Waste Land" in an exuberant voice.

Music was another great love of his. It played a much more important part in his life than most people realize, and a significant look into his orderly mind is found in his preferences: the delicate, highly disciplined fugues of Bach and Scarlatti, rather than the thundering works of Berlioz and other more bombastic composers. He especially was fond of Beethoven's Ninth Symphony and even established it as a "must" rendition at the UN day concerts. Hammarskjold never studied any instrument formally, but regarded listening to music as an art in its own right. Some aides believed that Bach's Brandenburg Concertos helped him through the more tense and crucial episodes of the Suez emergency.

Hammarskjold was also an exceptionally gifted connoiseur of painting. His tastes, almost rigidly modern, could be seen in his office. When he first moved in, he wanted to redecorate the suite, but was hampered by the Secretariat's drum-tight budget. (For some time, the only item of decor in the office was a leopard skin rug, a gift from admirers in Nigeria). He mentioned this one day to architect Wallace K. Harrison, one of the designers of the UN building. Within hours, Harrison had spoken to friends at New York's Museum of Modern Art. They immediately offered the indefinite loan of whatever paintings the Secretary-General might care to select. Soon, works by Picasso, Braque and Gris were adorning Hammarskjold's office walls. There were also a few drawing and paintings by prominent Swedish modernists - as well as a picture of Columbus' "Santa Maria." A friend said that Hammarskjold liked to compare Columbus' first voyage to the UN's great navigation effort, "Despairing and horrorful, full of trust and courage."

The 38th floor was not the only part of the UN

building where Hammarskjold's taste in art was reflected. During the height of the Suez crisis, he somehow found the time to supervise personally the remodelling of the UN "Meditation Room". The predominant feature of this quiet, serene non-sectarian chapel is its "altar" — a six-ton slab of Swedish iron ore illuminated from above by a single shaft of light. And on at least one occasion, the Secretary-General's preoccupations with art involved him in small diplomatic wrangles. When the Yugoslav government presented the UN with a handsome bronze figure, its delegation got into a heated argument with building officials over where the figure should be located. Hammarskjold stepped into the breach with the finesse of an ambassador and the instinct of an artist. Choosing a "neutral" spot in the UN gardens, he explained that the site was on a direct axis with several famous New York landmarks, and that the sculpture would therefore be the most conspicuous object in the courtyard. The Yugoslavs accepted the Secretary-General's recommendation enthusiastically.

It was at his home, however, that Hammarskjold's taste was most apparent. Restful simplicity was the predominant feature of his eight-room duplex apartment on Park Avenue. It was Hammarskjold himself, assisted by Swedish architect Andreas Bjorklund, who supervised the overall layout, and he obviously found a lot of pleasure in the task. Every room was strikingly handsome, but with a total absence of ostentation. Most

The Secretary-General in his New York City apartment

of the Danish and Swedish furniture – made to Hammarskjold's own specifications – had the economical, clean-cut lines that characterize modern Scandinavian design. The floor of the hall was decorated with patterns in colored tile. Draperies and upholstery were of a red Swedish damask. The works of Swedish contemporary painters adorned the walls. In fact, the whole atmosphere of the apartment was thoroughly Scandinavian.

A friend said: "I hardly think that you could find a more beautiful Swedish home in the United States."

Hammarskjold sometimes entertained chiefs of state, ambassadors, and UN delegates at formal dinners in his apartment. On these occasions, he refused to give any information to the press, not even a guest list. Generally, however, his official duties as host were more public, and consisted of receptions in the great lounge on the second floor of the Secretariat. If the gathering should be smaller and less formal, Hammarskjold invited his guests to his 38th-floor office suite, with its splendid view of the city.

Official receptions and dinners were a necessary part of Hammarskjold's duty, a duty which he performed impeccably, for he was a superb host in the best continental manner. And, as a uniquely eligible bachelor ("McCall's" once cited him among the 24 most charming men of the world) he could have been a leading figure in New York society if he wished. But he turned down party invitations with clocklike regularity. He accepted the public aspects of his responsibility as Secretary-General, but guarded his personal identity to a point where it even caused him inconvenience.

For example, although he liked to attend the theater, he hated to do so because of the attention he invariably drew. Giving up the theater was a sacrifice to him, because Hammarskjold's knowledge of drama was comprehensive and almost professional. (In fact, through his

[159]

personal friendship with Karl Ragnar, director of Sweden's Royal Theatre of Dramatic Arts, and with relatives of the late Eugene O'Neill, he was instrumental in arranging the Swedish productions of "Long Day's Journey Into Night" and "A Touch of the Poet,")

Despite a twenty-thousand-dollar tax-free salary and a thirty-five-thousand-dollar expense allowance, Hammarskjold's private social life consisted largely of playing host at small informal dinners for personal friends. In his personal circle of friends painters, writers and musicians easily outnumbered diplomats. Leonard Bernstein, Pablo Casals, Fritz Kreisler, Alfred H. Barr John Steinbeck and their wives all were guests at the New York apartment. Conversation was the principal attraction at these private gatherings, with good food a close second.

Hammarskjold himself ate sparingly, but his instincts were those of a gourmet. He liked to prepare exotic and elaborate variations on the Smorgasbord theme for his guests. In fact, he often gave his cook a night off at such gatherings. He also personally selected every vintage wine in his wine closet.

Hammarskjold was not an easy man to know. A UN associate once said that "he chooses his friends with the same meticulous care he puts into the selection of a modern painting". But he did enjoy unusually warm and lasting relations with a handful of people, some of whom he knew from his childhood in Sweden. Whenever he and any of these old companions met for a reunion, Hammarskjold unbent completely and reminisced about student days in Stockholm. The gatherings often wound up in badly-harmonized welter of university songs.

In this tight and somewhat exclusive circle, Hammarskjold was known for his thoughtfulness. He never failed to remember a birthday, anniversary or other personal occasion. A friend once said, "It's a wonder that he still has time to do it all. No one would blame him if he forgot his social duties. But even in the middle of some burning crisis, he still has time to look back toward Sweden daily. Telegrams and telephone conversations constantly link the two shores of the Atlantic. He will briefly say, 'I have been a little busy lately, as you may have seen in the papers . . .' On the exact day, a relative will receive his birthday present, a sick friend an encouraging note, an old schoolmate will be remembered with a couple of tickets for the meeting of the Swedish Academy, or he will go out and personally select a book for the wife of one of his associates."

And surprisingly — except to his friends — he was an unusually sentimental man. A death or illness caused him personal and prolonged distress. UN colleagues were invariably amazed when this little-known side of his character appeared. "The man becomes positively maudlin," a British correspondent once declared.

This was the indoor Hammarskjold — the cultivated intellectual, the modestly gracious host, the quiet, faithful friend. The more rugged side of his personality was not as well known.

Despite the cultured, scholarly atmosphere in which he grew up, Dag was an ardent devotee of what Theodore Roosevelt called "the strenuous life". At 56 he was in far better physical shape than most men twenty years younger. He seemed almost totally immune to sickness - even a toothache or mild cold - and never suffered in the slightest from any of the strange foods he often had to eat, especially in the tropics.

From time to time, friends heard him complain that he could seldom get away for more than an occasional weekend to his 80-acre estate in Brewster, N.Y. This was a sort of personal Shangri-la, tucked deep in the heavily wooded foothills of the Catskills. When Hammarskjold did manage to escape from the city and spend a few days here, he went another personality transformation in the sharp mountain air. At Brewster, he could get into faded khaki slacks and sneakers, roll up the sleeves of his old plaid jacket and take off on what he called as a "mammoth" hike through the hills. On these brief holidays, he lived mostly on canned foods and simple fare.

His day at Brewster usually began about an hour before sunrise, when everyone had to get up and eat a breakfast of bacon, canned beans, and coffee, followed by a six or seven-hour hike and informal nature study session. Hammarskjold led the way at a relentless pace, stopping only occasionally - to follow the flight of a bird, to drop on hands and knees and examine a rare species of caterpillar, or to photograph a scenic panorama with his camera. After lunch (usually bacon and beans again, topped off with coffee flavored ice cream), his guests were free to collapse for the rest of the afternoon if they wished. Hammarskjold himself generally went off on another tramp.

Sometimes the pattern varied. Instead of a mere morning hike, Dag occasionally decided on a two-day camping trip, equipped with little more than a tent and full supply of the inevitable tinned foods. Hammarskjold did all the work on these jaunts. He chose the campsite, pitched the tent, chopped the firewood, drew the water, cooked all the meals, and even washed the tin plates and knives. A reporter once remarked, "If Dag ever gets fed up at the UN, he can always go to work as a scoutmaster."

Bicycling was another pastime which he practiced. Once, shortly before World War II, he spent an entire day cycling through the countryside not far from Stockholm in a torrential downpour. Arriving at a small village, he went to the local hotel and asked for a room. The clerk, not recognizing the boyish-looking guest with the rucksack, uncombed hair, and mud-spattered shorts, suggested, "Boy, better try a youth hotel," which the Chairman of the Bank of Sweden promptly did.

The outdoor activity to which Hammarskjold was most passionately devoted—mountain climbing—was one for which he had little time after he became Secretary-General. Mountain climbing is unequaled in the degree of skill and courage it requires, in its extreme danger and unparalleled reward. To a true alpinist, mountaineering is far more than mere recreation; it is a way of life. Hammarskjold was one of the most dedicated and respected of the genuinely skilled practitioners of the art, and at one time was chairman of the

Dag and Premier Adoula listening to the Congo national anthem

Swedish Mountaineering Club.

In 1959, he became one of the few persons who ever received official permission from the Nepalese government to photograph Mount Everest and its surrounding ranges from the air. The Himalayas are holy to the people

[164]

of this country, and foreigners are expected to display proper reverence and respect for the great peaks. Government authorities arranged the flight while Hammarskjold was on a UN mission to Nepal. He later described his experience in an article in the *National Geographic* magazine, illustrated with the gripping color photographs he took from the cabin of an old DC-3.

This was no ordinary air journey. Flying over the "roof of the world" - with its unpredictable and savage air currents, with the ever present threat of being "closed in" by sudden fog, snow, hail, or sleet - can be nearly as perilous as an assault on one of the towering summits. Hammarskjold's account of the flight provided a rare insight into his character. In one passage he was the practical, veteran mountaineer: ". . . as we came closer, my climber's instincts were aroused and I started speculating, in vain, on possible routes of access for those who might one day brave this most inaccessible south mountain wall . . ." In another passage he was the ordinary human being, who suddenly becomes aware of danger: ". . . we had lost altitude, and I could not help smiling - perhaps a little apprehensively - when I saw the pilot looking down through a side window to judge if he would get safely over the range we had to pass . . ." And above all, he was the visionary and poet: ". . . we suddenly had before us Annapurna, with a beauty of structure and a majesty far surpassing that of Everest or Gauri Sandar. It seemed . . . built by the gods for their incarnation not as frail human beings but as giants.

The contrast between the sovereign quiet of the mountaintop and the wild ranges leading in toward it added to the other-worldliness, the feeling that we had penetrated into a world of cosmic purpose and character."

Many other intriguing clues to Hammarskjold's complex personality - both in private life and in the UN - can be found in his love for mountaineering. Wilfrid Noyce, one of the team that reached the summit of Everest in 1953, later wrote an article entitled "Why Men Climb Mountains." In it, he said, "If you would really know a person, there is no better device than to climb with him on the same rope, to be overtaken by night together on the same tiny cold ledge with no food. Then you will know better whether he is your friend than if you have spent twenty summers playing golf together, or if he is 'always such good company' at cocktail parties . . . .In a high camp your friend of sea level may turn into a positive ogre . . . If you can go on enjoying the same person's mountain company, in any part of the world, for more than ten years, then he is your friend indeed." This, in a sense, describes Hammarskjold's own mountaineer's attitude in forming friendships. His friends were few and meticulously chosen, but they were enduring.

Noyce has something else to say, "Climbing with one or two others, you are no longer a single person, you are a 'party', or when there are a number of climbers, an 'expedition.' You move as one, feel as one; sometimes your very life depends on your thinking as one. I like the

[*166*]

sensation that the rope joining me to my friend is more than a physical bond; it is the reason two small human beings are able to overcome the hugeness of the confronting mountain, and to climb together one degree neared the stars." Seldom has a clearer picture been drawn of Dag Hammarskjold's feeling about the UN mission. He viewed it as an "expedition" – a task of international teamwork in which all the members are not competing, or even operating independently, but striving as a single entity toward an identical goal.

There was considerable significance in one article of decoration on the living room wall in Hammarskjold's Park Avenue apartment. It was an ice axe, presented to him by Tenzing Norkay, the Sherpa guide who took part in the 1953 Everest climb. With the axe is a note which reads, "So that you may climb to greater heights."

Chapter **11**

The "Impossible Job"

One of the unspoken requirements for the job of UN Secretary-General is that he be willing to be a target. After assuming office in 1953, Dag Hammarskjold was on the receiving end of unfriendly gestures from nearly every member-nation of the world body. The barbs leveled at him ranged from the courteous but clear disapproval expressed by the United States during the Hungarian crisis, to the savage and almost obscene personal abuse bellowed by Nikita Khrushchev.

Such hostility has to be expected. It is simply an occupational hazard that goes with the job of being the world's number one peacemaker. Hammarskjold seemed to realize this and always handled each angry member nation with impeccable tact.

Many of Hammarskjold's difficulties arose from

matters in which he was not even involved. For example, in August, 1961, Michel Collet, a member of the Guinean delegation to the UN, was involved in a minor traffic accident while driving through New York's Harlem district. When police arrived on the scene, a scuffle started, and Delegate Collet was taken to the nearest police station. There he angrily announced to reporters that he was a victim of "discrimination" and "police brutality," that the police had jumped him and slugged him mercilessly because he was black.

When the story got out, the Guinean delegation launched a furious protest, and demanded a full-scale investigation.

By the time it reached Dag Hammarskjold's desk the story had been exaggerated, and had resulted in ill feelings, toward the United States. The Afro-Asian group, in a body, called on the Secretary-General to demand that "self-respect, dignity, and freedom from racial discrimination" be accorded UN diplomats here.

This was "characteristic," raged the protest, of the "treatment received by Africans in neo-colonialistic countries." A special committee of Afro-Asian bloc delegates was formed to investigate the incident. UN Ambassador Stevenson hastily conveyed official regrets to the Guinean government. The story was trumpeted with grim delight in Moscow. Cairo radio flashed it out on short-wave, and hundreds of millions of non-whites all over the world were told of the newest atrocity perpetrated by America's "race-baiting" policemen.

[169]

Meanwhile, the police had prepared their own report, on orders from New York's Mayor Robert F. Wagner. The report stated that Delegate Collet had been arrested only after he assaulted the traffic officers. Because Monsieur Collet was reported to have a quick temper, Mayor Wagner accepted the report, and so did the Afro-Asian committee. The Guinean delegation emitted a few more growls, and the matter seemed to have been finally dropped. But the damage had been done. As usual, Dag Hammarskjold had been in the middle.

Incidents like these affect United Nations prestige. In an organization staffed by persons from many different countries there is always the possibility of spying, sabotage or counter-espionage. By treaty with the United States, United Nations members are granted special privileges and immunities in connection with their office and they occupy a unique - and often delicate - relation to the people of New York and the United States. When a man named Igor Melekh, a Soviet citizen employed by the Secretariat, was indicted for espionage, a loud and angry furor developed over the question of his status. Could he or could he not claim diplomatic immunity? As a UN Secretariat employee he could not, even if he claimed that he had also retained his status in the Soviet Foreign Ministry. When a Yugoslav delegate accidentally ran over and killed a pedestrian on New York's West Side, the same question arose. Neither case helped the stature of the UN in popular opinion.

One of Hammarskjol's never-ending headaches

was the job of finding apartments for African delegates and Secretariat employes. Most New York realtors will simply not rent to them, using the flimsiest and shabbiest of excuses. As a result, many top officials of African governments often have to make a choice between a prohibitively expensive hotel suite or a slum apartment in Harlem. The Soviets were alert to every instance of bigotry and exploited them to the hilt, frequently holding Dag responsible.

However, the Communists were by no means the exclusive source of attacks on the Secretary-General. Hammarskjold was also a favorite target of the right-wing radicals, especially the John Birch Society, which characterized him as "one of the most contemptible agents of the Kremlin ever supported by the American taxpayers." Spokesmen of the right wing stepped up the tempo of their anti-Hammarskjold barrage after the case of Denmark's Paul Bang-Jensen became the UN's biggest unsolved mystery.

The story began in January, 1957, when Bang-Jensen was appointed Deputy Secretary of the UN Special Committee on the problem of Hungary. The group, visiting five European cities, took testimony from witnesses about the Soviet invasion of Budapest in October of 1956.

"Of the 111 witnesses . . ." an official report stated, "81 requested leave to testify anonymously. In every case the request was granted without question. They were entitled to the shelter of the anonymity which they sought, and they received it." Bang-Jensen kept the secret names in his possession, and in August returned to his regular duties in the Department of Political and Security Council Affairs.

The following October, a U.S. State Department inquiry, addressed to Hammarskjold, started a new train of events. The inquiry concerned a Hungarian refugee who had testified before the Special Committee the previous winter. The only person who knew his identity was Bang-Jensen, and he refused to reveal the refugee's name. Hammarskjold insisted that Bang-Jensen turn over the list of names, and Bang-Jensen refused. In December, he was suspended from his job, and Hammarskjold appointed a legal committee to investigate Bang-Jensen's actions.

On January 24, 1958, Bang-Jensen went to the roof of the UN building and burned the list of 81 names in the presence of witnesses.

Shortly afterwards, the legal committee appointed by Hammarskjold concluded its investigation and recommended that Bang-Jensen be dismissed. Bang-Jensen, in return, filed an appeal. A drawn-out legal battle started and finally came to an end in December, when his final appeal to the Administrative Tribunal was rejected.

On Thanksgiving Day, 1959, Paul Bang-Jensen was found dead in a park in Queens, New York. The autopsy report read, "Cause of death: gunshot wound of the head; suicidal."

Quickly a rumor circulated that the "suicide" had

been arranged by the Russians, old hands at the tactic of liquidation. To many people, in fact, the circumstances of Bang-Jensen's death have never been satisfactorily explained. But there was no question in the minds of many John Birch Society members. They not only stated outright that Bang-Jensen was murdered, but that the ultimate responsibility for his death lay with Dag Hammarskjold's himself. Birch Society President Robert Welch, referring to the legal battle in the UN, said that there was no chance for justice to be done "once Dag Hammarskjold had made it clear to his sycophantic subordinates that Bang-Jensen was marked for destruction."

None of the abuse that Dag Hammarskjold received, from either left or right, was likely to hurt the veteran mountaineer personally. But it did make "the impossible job" just a little more so.

Chapter *12*

Epitaph for a Soldier of Peace

In June, 1961, a cartoon appeared in a Washington newspaper. It showed Nikita Khrushchev standing outside the UN building with Mao Tse Tung, who had long sought to have Red China's admitted to the world group. Khrushchev, an axe in his hand, was saying, "Listen, when we get through with it, it won't be worth belonging to."

Russian attacks against the UN had increased about twelve months previously, during the 1960 Congo emergency. The Russians hoped this crisis would enable them to gain a foothold on the African continent. Since stepping up the attack, Khrushchev had gone to the mat twice with Hammarskjold. On both occasions he had been thrown decisively. By early 1961, after the U.S.S.R.'s second defeat, it had become painfully clear that the

Secretary-General was the chief obstacle in the way of Soviet ambitions. Russia's course was clear: Hammarskjold must be removed.

The Soviet plan was simple enough. They proposed to do away with Hammarskjold's job and replace him with a three-man directorate representing East, West, and neutral blocs. This machinery, the Russians claimed, would be more workable and assure more equitable and mutually satisfactory decisions for all member-nations. The Soviet apparatus was nicknamed the "troika," after the three-horse teams commonly used in Russia.

Few, if any, non-communist nations were fooled by the alleged efficiency of this weird three-headed Secretary-General - or by the Soviet motives in proposing it. But the Russians' failure to delude the rest of the world did not make their proposal any less dangerous.

The Soviets knew that the "troika" proposal, by its very existence, could easily open the door to attacks on other executive functions of the Secretariat. In fact, the Russians themselves led this assault, demanding that all of the more than one thousand Secretariat appointments be made under a "troika" system.

For Dag Hammarskjold the Red pattern was only too clear. With opposing ideological blocs replacing impartial representation within the Secretariat, the entire UN machinery could rapidly be brought to a standstill. The "troika" concept, he declared, was a blatant violation of the Charter. As for the Soviet demand that all Secretariat positions be allocated on a political basis - again the "troika" in another disguise - he pointed out the elementary difference between members of the Secretariat and delegates from individual nations. Secretariat employees, he said, are bound by the Charter to serve the organization, not the policies of their own countries.

He went even further, and reminded the Soviets that he had been trying to bring Iron Curtain Secretariat membership up to quota for years. The only thing that had prevented him, he added, was the Russians themselves. They had consistently blocked the appointment of genuinely qualified men for the Secretariat positions that were open.

These comments — made early in July of 1961 — were part of his reply to the recommendations of a review board which had been seeking methods of reorganizing the Secretariat. Hammarskjold accepted certain of the recommendations, and made some suggestions of his own. He said he wished to see fourteen new subordinate secretaries, five holding "political" posts and nine functioning in an "administrative" capacity. One of the "political" offices would go to a Russian, and one to an American. The other three were to go to citizens "outside any power bloc".

With this plan, Hammarskjold hoped to counter the Russian proposal. Yet Hammarskjold knew his reorganization program might turn out to be little more than a holding action. The Soviets, he realized, would not give up without a terrific fight in the Assembly.

It was for this reason that when the Secretary-General's Annual Report was published in August, Hammarskjold's introduction dealt directly with the alarming cleavage within the world body. This "state of the UN message" was a masterful reply to the Russians and their fellow-obstructionists. Hammarskjold made it crystal-clear that he was not defending the UN—he was counter-attacking. And he lost no time in getting to the point.

The report started off by declaring that among member-nations, two opposing views of the UN had emerged. One was that the organization was simply "static conference machinery". The other view was that the organization was a "parliament," with an equal vote for every member. The "conference" idea, said Hammarskjold, might manage to keep the world from war—with luck—but it could never eliminate the specter of a perpetual armed truce. The "parliament," with all its imperfections, could ultimately remove the fears and suspicions which prevent true world peace.

What about these conflicting views as they applied to the Secretariat? Hammarskjold was equally clear here. Whenever the situation might demand initiative on the part of the Secretary-General, he should have authority to take it. Indeed, he pointed out, that authority already existed, not only by virtue of precedent but under the Charter itself.

As for the "troika" scheme, he had this to say, ". . . while no man is neutral in the sense that he is without opinions or ideals, it is just as true that . . . a neutral secretariat is possible. Anyone of integrity, not subjected to undue pressures, can, regardless of his own views, readily act in an 'exclusively international' spirit . . ."

The report was not neutral. It was not intended to be. Hammarskjold saw that the UN's very life was at stake, and he stated his own views clearly and emphatically. As he saw it, the "static conference", supported by the Soviets and their allies, was totally inconsistent with the aims of the UN's "founding fathers." If adopted, it could reduce the world group to the helpless level of the old League of Nations. The "dynamic" approach, however, not only gave the Charter a new set of teeth; it represented the world's greatest hope for an ultimate end to all war.

He didn't mince words, either, as to the consequences of obstructionist tactics of the Russians. "Those whose reactions to the work of the organization hamper its development or reduce its possibilities of effective action, may have to shoulder the responsibility for a return to a state of affairs which Governments had already found too dangerous after the First World War."

Hammarskjold's unusually plain-spoken report amounted to a declaration of faith in a strong, dynamic world parliament for peace. It could not have been put more courteously, but the meaning was inescapable: It's up to you, gentlemen. It's your United Nations, to do with as you choose. You can make it into a dynamic, meaningful instrument which, despite its human short-

[178]

comings, can some day bring lasting peace to the world. Or, if you choose, you can smash it, to achieve petty ends and satisfy petty jealousies, and in so doing you will probably smash the entire world. The choice is yours, gentlemen, and there is not much time.

Time was running out. It had been scarcely a year since Khrushchev and the satellite leaders stood up in the General Assembly and launched their opening barrage of personal abuse against the Secretary-General. And despite two stinging rebuffs, they appeared ready to lash out once again with even more fury.

Shortly before the 16th General Assembly session, the Russians shocked the world by resuming nuclear tests. This was particularly appalling to the twenty-five neutral or "nonaligned" nations which had just assembled for a major conference in Belgrade. Many neutrals had leaned toward the Communist position; others were outright supporters. Now the neturals began to take a new look.

Yet even the possibility of near-total world alignment against the Iron Curtain did not seem to faze Khrushchev. He himself had said that he recognized no neutrals. The approaching clash would inevitably find Dag Hammarskjold in the middle once again.

Too, there was the question of Red China. For years, the United States had effectively blocked debate on that nation's admission to membership in the UN. Now it was obvious that the United States could no longer control sufficient votes on the issue. Hammarskjold knew that Red China's membership would provide the Soviets with an ally of fantastic power and influence. He knew that Khrushchev and Mao Tse Tung would be certain to gang up on the Secretary-General, and continue the Communist effort to wreck the UN. But as the rigidly impartial administrator of the organization, Hammarskjold would do nothing to prevent debate, vote, or even admission of Red China.

Berlin loomed as another threat to peace. The Reds had literally built an iron curtain around the Soviet-controlled sector of the city. Russian tanks and troops patrolled the border to freedom. U.S. forces faced them in the west zone. The situation was perfect for an explosion. Could the UN prevent an outbreak of violence?

There was also Bizerte. The question of French bases in Tunisia had touched off savage brush-fire battles in August, and although France and Tunisia subsequently came closer to settlement of the dispute, the conflict had brought an ugly problem into the open. French president De Gaulle made no bones about his contempt for the UN, and he made it clear he would refuse to accept its recommendations unless they suited his aims. Many observers considered De Gaulle's hostile stubbornness as dangerous as the Russian intransigence; some even feared that France might leave the UN entirely.

There were many "insignificant" headaches that also promised to plague the Secretary-General. Typical was the question of Alto Adige, a small community in northern Italy, populated largely by Austrians who had long been demanding union with their native land – or autonomy at least. Disorders and violence in Alto Adige were bound to result in the problem being put on the Assembly agenda. This was merely one of innumerable small problems – trifling matters individually, but colossal when taken together.

The most serious crisis was still the Congo. Things had started to go badly there again. For some weeks, it had begun to look as if the turmoil in that tortured land might be ending. But suddenly, almost overnight, a rash of violence broke out savagely. Moise Tshombe, political leader of Katanga province, reverted to his stubborn position of "independence," and rejected the central government's demand – supported by the United Nations – that the Belgian officers and foreign mercenaries of Katanga's armed forces be dismissed. In Elizabethville, the provincial capital, fierce fighting broke out between Katanga and UN troops. Cyrille Adoula, newly-elected premier of the Congo, prepared to send a strong expeditionary force from Leopoldville. Tshombe disappeared. The fighting spread from Elizabethville to the north and west. Once more, the strife-torn Equatorial nation tottered on the brink of a civil war that could easily become a world conflagration.

The Katanga crisis could not have taken place at a worse time for the free world. However, the Russians characteristically looked on this threat to peace as a stroke of luck. They lost no time in seizing it as an opening wedge for their assault on the world organization.

Hammarskjold, out of painful experience, knew that he must act swiftly. With only a few days remaining before the opening of the 16th Assembly, there was little time to attend to this brush-fire war and still take care of the thousands of details involved with the opening of the Assembly. With his characteristic decisiveness, Hammarskjold once again turned to Bill Ranallo, his trusted aide, and told him to meet him with his ever-ready bag and camera. They were flying to the Congo.

Shortly after midnight on September 18, 1961, a voice with a heavy Scandinavian accent came through the speaker in the control tower of the airport at Ndola, a small town in the "Copperbelt" of Northern Rhodesia, only a few miles from the Congo border. The British operations officer peered out into the night. Despite the murk, he could see that the runway was clear. In a flat, official monotone, he "talked" the plane down to 6,000 feet, and gave final landing instructions. A few seconds later he heard the sound of an aircraft circling the field.

"Overdue by ninety minutes," he remarked to the radio operator at the control board. "But better late than never, what?"

Then, inexplicably, the sound of the plane's engines faded out.

"That's odd," said the radio operator. "Wonder what happened."

Down on the field, at the edge of the apron, a small group of UN and British officials looked at one another

[182]

in puzzled anxiety. They had been waiting since 10:30 for the DC-6B which was carrying Dag Hammarskjold and his staff from Leopoldville. It had finally arrived — and then vanished.

By sunrise, a small air armada was skirting low over the central African bush — searching . . .

Moise Tshombe had persistently scorned UN action ever since he took over as Katanga's "strong man." Nevertheless, he held a deep respect for Hammarskjold's office. Now, on September 18, he was holding a press conference. Hammarskjold, he told newsmen, was due to arrive any moment, and he voiced his confidence that their talks would bring an end to Katanga's violence. A reporter entered the room.

"President Tshombe," he said, "Mr Hammarskjold is dead."

Search planes had spotted the smoking wreckage of the DC-6B from the air, but the rescue party had to hack its way through the bush to reach the scene of the tragedy. When they arrived, they found only one survivor, Harold M. Julian, a UN security guard. Although critically injured, he was able to give a partly coherent account of the terrible catastrophe. Just after landing clearance had been received from the Ndola tower, said Julian, Hammarskjold ordered the pilot to remain airborne and change course. It was not clear whether the Secretary-General had given these orders immediately before or after a series of explosions rocked the aircraft. Nor was it clear whether there had been engine trouble, whether the plane had been attacked by one of Katanga's two jet fighters, or whether there had been sabotage.

Harold Julian died a few days later. He had been under heavy sedation and had been unable to supply any additional information. Now there was no longer a survivor to furnish a clue to the tragedy.

But one awful fact could not be questioned.

Not since Franklin D. Roosevelt's death in 1945 had the world been so stunned. While messages of condolence poured in from every nation, the delegates to the General Assembly convened. They listened to the eulogies for Dag Hammarskjold in what seemed a state of shock. They had gathered in New York to deal with an alarming threat to peace. Nearly all of them had looked for leadership in this struggle to the polite, impartial—and astonishingly strong—personality who had guided the UN through so many crises. Now, as the session began, they could only stand in silence and mourn him. The rostrum of the UN Assembly seemed suddenly to be transformed into a funeral bier. There was no coffin—only an empty chair and the remembrance of a man who had sat there for eight years and whose presence—ear-phones, cigarillo, and solemn face—made itself felt to every delegate. How he would have hated all those words of eulogy, this man who shunned the personal adjective.

The next days, as the shock subsided, a thousand editorials acclaimed the stature of the sandy-haired

The Security Council meets to mourn Hammarskjold's death

Swede who reached his summit with such meteoric speed. For weeks the eulogies flowed from every corner of the globe. It seemed like an overwhelming negation of that old English saying that "... When you die, your trumpeter will be buried." At the United Nations, it seemed that the delegates could not recover from the loss, even though new names were being talked of a Dag's successor.

The Russians apparently were the first to recover from the shock of Hammarskjold's death. They had joined in the world-wide expressions of condolence, although callously persisting in their refusal to refer to Hammarskjold – even in death – by the title of Secretary-General. Now they knew that they could waste no time in seizing the opportunity that had arisen from the tragedy. Without Hammarskjold, the UN was in the most precarious position in its history. This was Russia's greatest chance to make the world body the instrument of Soviet designs.

They began to eye the Congo again, throwing around the familiar charges of "colonialism," "copper capitalists," and "tools of imperialism." They revived the "troika" plan. Hammarskjold's firmness had foiled the "troika" scheme earlier, but now the way was clear for the Soviets to make another try, and with renewed and unrelenting fury. If a strong, tough Secretary-General could be replaced by a directorate of three figureheads representing power blocs, and with vetoes in their pockets, a new and unthinkable kind of anarchy would result. And sixteen years of dedicated work toward genuine world harmony would be crushed beneath the iron wheels of another Soviet vehicle – the one they call "the locomotive of history."

Most nations were resolved that the UN must not be destroyed. One of the first to step into the void of leadership was the United States. President Kennedy, in a forceful address to the General Assembly, told the delegates that however difficult it was going to be to replace Hammarskjold, it was better to replace him with one man than with three. "Even the three horses of the troika did not have three drivers, all going in different directions," the President said. A detonation of applause indicated a fierce determination to resist the Soviet sabotage. And if they did, it would be due almost entirely to the strength which Dag Hammarskjold had instilled in the world body.

Under his guidance, the Assembly had evolved from an ineffectual debating society of 50 nations into a focal point of world opinion and conscience. Since 1953, membership had nearly doubled. The emergence of independent African nations had created a new and powerful bloc of neutral states which could play a significant part in molding the future of the world for good — or for evil. These nations, along with the slightly older free states of Asia, had come to wield the balance of power which formerly swerved between the Iron Curtain and the West. Often, it is true, the neutrals had used this influence as a weapon, playing the Free World against the Communists for whatever they might be able to get out of it in technical and financial assistance. More recently, however, they had come to show a new maturity, a deeper sense of the significance of their responsibility. This sense of responsibility could go far in strengthening the United Nations itself.

The General Assembly, when all is said and done, has no power at all in the conventional sense of the word.

It does not legislate. It cannot issue commands. Its recommendations are no more binding than the moral force behind them. Yet if the organization is respected by all nations – particularly the nonaligned states – the power of abstract ideals will take on more meaning and value than ever before in history. And it was Dag Hammarskjold who, almost alone, brought the Assembly from the discussion group stage to threshold of real power. It was Dag Hammarskjold who gave the body an active, forceful, and increasingly respected function.

He accomplished what he did mainly in two ways. One was through the creation of UN "armies" which were often attacked and sometimes even defeated. But at no time could any nation – even the Soviet Union – ignore the fact that the troops represented no individual interest or ambition. They were on hand only to keep the peace. As such, and in their purely international character, they became a symbol of the world's conscience.

Hammarskjold's other principal method of strengthening the UN was by raising the office of Secretary-General from that of mere administrator to a position of enormous influence and power. Trygve Lie had been unable to do this, partly because he did not have the votes of the smaller Asian-African nations which subsequently became available to Hammarskjold.

But Hammarskjold's own rugged determination cannot be overlooked as one of the key factors in the new stature of the Secretariat. If the UN was to be a real spokesman for the rule of law, it had to have strength and direction from the top. This meant a Secretary-General willing and able to accept responsibility, to act quickly and decisively whenever the threat of war arose, and above all, to maintain an unceasing impartiality.

It was this latter accomplishment, more than anything else, which brought Hammarskjold to his last-ditch battle with the nations that sought to destroy the UN. And, in a curious way, his greatest monument may be the blind fury of the assaults that were leveled against him. When he put teeth into the Charter, it was inevitable that some countries would be bitten. And when Hammarskjold faced the storm of their rage, he personified the United Nations in action.

Adlai Stevenson asked that Hammarskjold be buried on the site of the United Nations, "by the river at this headquarters of the organization to which he gave his life." This did not happen. Hammarskjold's body was flown to Sweden. After a Lutheran church service, a royal funeral, and a torchlight procession in which thousands marched, his remains were interred in the family plot at Uppsala. Yet the location of his final resting place, or a statue to him on the grounds of the UN in New York, as was suggested—none of these matter too much. He would have agreed with Cato, *"I had rather men should ask why my statue is not set up, than why it is."* And he could have said it in pure Latin, too. What does matter is that in the hearts of men, women, and children

[*189*]

the world over, Dag Hammarskjold's presence has taken its rightful place – alongside the "UN presence," the idea he had conceived and implemented.

For those growing up in the Suspenseful Sixties, Hammarskjold's importance is that at the end of the sixteenth year of the United Nations he had emerged as a kind of colossus astride a war-weary, peace-longing world. His legacy was as an indelible guide-post – a monument, if one must have a monument – to a warless world. As James Reston pointed out, Hammarskjold had actually written his own epitaph. On his first trip to India as Secretary General he was watching some Hindu dances in the Lai Bagh Gardens. The dances were based on the theme of a poem by Sir Rabindranath Tagore:

"Listen to the rumbling of the clouds, O heart of mine. Be brave, break through and leave for the unknown ..."

Before Hammarskjold left India, he recommended this theme as a model for the United Nations itself.

"I think that these lines," he said, "express in a very noble way the attitude we must take to this venture called the United Nations. We may listen to the rumbling of the clouds, but we can never afford to lose that kind of confidence in ourselves and in wisdom of man which makes us brave enough to break through and leave, always leave for the unknown . . ."

Something he said when he took the oath as Secretary-General carried with it a suggestion of the sort of valedictory he himself might wish:

"This Organization [the UN] grew out of the pain and turmoil of the last war. It welded together all those who had fought against oppression. This organization, in the words of one of the great leaders of democracy 'Has been consecrated far above our poor power to add or detract.' Common to us all and above all other convictions, stands the truth once expressed by a Swedish poet when he said that the greatest prayer of man does not ask for victory – but for peace."